Roger S. Bagnall

EARLY CHRISTIAN
BOOKS IN EGYPT

Princeton University Press

Princeton and Oxford

Copyright © 2009 by Princeton University Press

Published by Princeton University Press, 41 William
Street, Princeton, New Jersey 08540

In the United Kingdom: Princeton University Press,
6 Oxford Street, Woodstock, Oxfordshire OX20 1TW

Library of Congress Cataloging-in-Publication Data

Bagnall, Roger S.
Early Christian books in Egypt / Roger S. Bagnall.
p. cm.
Includes bibliographical references (p.   ) and index.
ISBN 978-0-691-14026-1 (hardcover : alk. paper)
1. Christian literature, Early—Egypt—Manuscripts.
2. Egypt—Church history. 3. Manuscripts (Papyri)
I. Title.
BR190.B34 2009
276.2'01—dc22   2008045333

British Library Cataloging-in-Publication
Data is available

This book has been composed in Minion
Printed on acid-free paper. ∞
press.princeton.edu

Printed in the United States of America

1 3 5 7 9 10 8 6 4 2

For Henri Schiller

Contents

List of Figures

Preface

The four chapters of this book correspond to four lectures that I was privileged to deliver at the École Pratique des Hautes Études (5e section) in May 2006. The École Pratique has occupied a large place in my mental geography of the world of learning since a young age, when I spent many hours as a graduate student reading the collected articles of Louis Robert, including importantly his annual reports on his teaching there. I marveled then that there could be an institution where it was possible for such scholarship to be the material of teaching rather than merely of professorial research, and in the years that followed I have never ceased to admire the distinction of the work done there by many other luminaries. That this tradition should be continued in papyrology at the very highest level by the appointment of Jean-Luc Fournet was a great source of pleasure to me. I never imagined that I might one day be privileged, even if for a comparative instant, to appear in its roster of faculty, and I am grateful for the invitation to be a Directeur d'études invité.

As I remark in the first chapter, the subjects treated in these pages are hardly undiscovered terrain. Just in the year in which the lectures were delivered, two substantial books that might seem from their titles to cover much the same material were published (Grafton and Williams 2006; Hurtado 2006). And yet Hurtado (2006: 7) was moved to lament the degree to which the existence and character of the earliest Christian book fragments from Egypt are still widely unknown or underappreciated in the field of biblical studies. In any event, what I have tried to do in these four chapters is not to survey the subject again but to argue for the inadequacy of most of what has been said about several particular topics within this larger domain.[1]

The length of this book could easily have been tripled by adding anything resembling a full bibliography, and I have chosen to preserve the character of the lectures by keeping the bibliographic apparatus to a minimum. This will, however, lead the reader to much more extensive literature than what I cite directly while, as well, documenting specific statements in the text.

Probably no reader who has spent May in Paris will doubt my word that my wife, Whitney Bagnall, and I spent our four weeks in Paris very pleasantly. But even aside from the city's charms our stay owed much to the warmth of the hospitality we experienced there, and I take this opportunity to thank not only Jean-Luc Fournet, my host at EPHE, and his wife Caroline Magdelaine, but also Anne Boud'hors and Michel Garel, Jean-Michel Carrié, Mireille Corbier, Hélène Cuvigny and Adam Bülow-Jacobsen, Denis Feissel, Danielle Haase-Dubosc, Chantal Heurtel, Arietta Papaconstantinou and Jean-Claude Waquet, Delphine Renaut and Frederick Lauritzen, Suzanne Saïd, Henri Schiller, and Patricia Stirneman for sharing homes and meals with us. It was Mr. Schiller who originally suggested that I give these lectures, at that time intended to take place at the Bibliothèque nationale de France, and I dedicate the volume to him in thanks for our many years of friendship. I am particularly indebted to Danielle Haase-Dubosc for providing me with an office in Columbia University's Paris branch, Reid Hall, a luxury not provided by the EPHE even to its permanent faculty in its historic but cramped quarters.

Much of the content of the lectures had earlier been developed in the context of a graduate seminar at the University of California, Berkeley, when I was Sather Professor of Classical Literature in the fall of 2005. I am grateful to the members of that seminar for many helpful contributions to the development of my ideas; my particular indebtedness to Brendan Haug is noted in chapter 3. Sabine Hübner, who was a postdoctoral fellow with me that year on funds provided by the Andrew W. Mellon Foundation, was also an important contributor to some topics. In the final stages of editing, the book benefited from several astute observations by AnneMarie Luijendijk, to whom I am indebted for a careful reading of the manuscript, and by two press readers.

Like everything I wrote during my third of a century at Columbia University, this book is profoundly indebted to the Columbia University Libraries, their collections, services, and staff. I am grateful for their contributions to a productive working environment for scholarship in the humanities.

May 2008

A Note on Abbreviations

Papyri are cited according to *Checklist of Editions of Greek, Latin, Demotic and Coptic Papyri, Ostraca and Tablets,* ed. J. Oates et al., 5th ed. (BASP Supplement 9, 2001) (also available online and updated at http://scriptorium.lib.duke.edu/papyrus/texts/clist.html). References to LDAB, followed by numbers, refer to the Leuven Database of Ancient Books, online at http://www.trismegistos.org/ldab/.

EARLY CHRISTIAN
BOOKS IN EGYPT

CHAPTER I

The Dating of the Earliest
Christian Books in Egypt

GENERAL CONSIDERATIONS

The subject of this book, early Christian books in Egypt, cannot make any claim to novelty. The bibliography is enormous, and much of it is learned and even intelligent. If I dare to offer some observations on several aspects of this vast domain, it is certainly not because I think I know more about Christian literary manuscripts, or about book production in antiquity, or indeed about the dating of handwriting, than my predecessors. That is certainly not the case. Nor will many of my observations be very original. Rather, what has led me to trespass onto this intellectual territory is my unease with what I see as the excessively self-enclosed character and absence of self-awareness of much of that scholarship.

The narrowness of much of it has permitted its practitioners to reach conclusions that I believe are profoundly at odds with fundamental social realities of the ancient world and with basic probability; and the lack of a self-critical posture has been particularly damaging in that it has tended to allow problematic assumptions, interests, agendas, and desires to escape being made explicit. Much of what I have to say will therefore be directed at bringing these foundations of the discussion into the light and looking for their consequences. More broadly, my interest in the subject comes from two intersecting directions of work: first, social history and the role of writing in

ancient society; and second, the character of written texts as archaeological artifacts (Bagnall 1995).

The subject of early Christian books, of course, offers many in-
terpretations, many avenues of approach, and many sets of issues,
of which I shall deal with only a few. That there is such a diversity of
issues and approaches is in large part the result of Christianity's inheritance from Judaism of a writing-centered culture. I do not mean
by this to suggest that other characteristics of the religion, like ritual,
healings, and so on, were absent or unimportant, only that they were
perhaps less distinctive and original. The gospels and the letters of the
New Testament respond to certain characteristics of the early church
and embed its diversity and contentiousness. Surviving writings
that did not make their way into the eventual biblical canon go back
to almost as early a period as the gospels and epistles.[1] A religious
movement geographically dispersed around the Roman world, but
evidently, from an early date, intent on achieving some kind of unity
and uniformity, depended on correspondence and on written ver-
sions of its message to achieve any kind of coherence.[2] Such unity and
coherence need not have been important, but in Christianity clearly
they were felt to be important from the very beginning, or at least
from as close to it as we can get. This double drive for uniformity and
organizational structure is indeed one of Christianity's most distinctive characteristics.

It is particularly with the implications of surviving books and book
fragments for Christianity before Constantine that I shall be concerned, and especially with its first two centuries. That is where the
liveliest controversies are to be found. The reason for that is not ob-
scure. It is, quite simply, that we are far less well informed about pre-
Constantinian Christianity than we are about the fourth century or
later periods. This relative lack of information has been a central problem for scholarship, in large part because Christian discourse and the
study of Christianity have for more than a century been obsessed with
questions about the nature of early Christianity, of Christian "origins."[3] For modern scholars who were unfriendly to the Christianity
that emerged as catholic orthodoxy from the struggles of late antiquity it has been important to demonstrate that this late antique religion had betrayed the essence of the original message of the religion

it claimed to represent; and the contrary has been equally important to demonstrate for those intent on defending Nicene Christianity against all such assertions. The authority attributed by the church to Jesus and the canonical scriptures has been virtually the one element on which people who agree on little else can agree. Or, as we might put it, those who think that Nicene Christianity was a deviation from a more sympathetic primitive Christianity have adopted for the sake of persuasiveness a rhetorical strategy that privileges the supposed origins. Determining just what Jesus preached and how far the New Testament canon rests on an accurate rendering of that preaching has thus been one of the most durable of scholarly industries.

There is, of course, a large body of surviving extracanonical Christian writings from the period before Constantine, both those preserved and revered in orthodoxy and those rejected by it (Ehrman 2003). Many of the latter, although not all of them, were not transmitted in the medieval manuscript tradition and are known only from texts discovered since the late nineteenth century. The publication of the Gospel of Judas in April 2006 has brought one more element to this dossier.[4] But because all these writings, whether preserved or rejected by the church authorities, are with hardly an exception writings devoted to supporting one side or another of some ancient controversy, and thus obviously not objective witnesses to the early character of Christianity, there is a tradition, now of some antiquity itself, of looking to archaeological and documentary sources—using these terms in a broad sense—to try to capture a less tendentious and more "authentic" early Christianity.[5] That notion is itself problematic, but that is not my subject here.

In that endeavor, Egyptian Christianity has played a central role, mainly because the survival of papyri there seemed already by the early twentieth century to offer hopes of recovering an earlier documentary past than was available elsewhere, but also because the episcopal throne of Alexandria was one of the most prestigious of late antiquity and seemed to demand a past commensurate with its distinction and influence under Athanasius and his successors. And even for the period after Constantine, when archaeological evidence remains relatively scarce until the fifth century, the evidence from the papyri has continued to be called on to help us figure out what was going on behind the noisy clash of doctrines in the theological literature, above all what were the realities of daily practice and habits (Wipszycka 1996, 2007a, and forthcoming).

The pressure to produce usable information from the papyri has been even more intense than it might otherwise have been precisely because Christianity before Constantine in Egypt itself is so poorly known from the literary tradition. There is in effect a vast blank, the "mere echo and a puff of smoke" as Walter Bauer famously called it.[6] Most of this tiny amount of traditional information comes from Eusebius's *Church History*, and it does not give one the impression that Eusebius knew a lot. In book 2, chapter 16, he says, "They say that this Mark was the first to be sent to preach in Egypt the gospel which he had also put into writing, and was the first to establish churches in Alexandria itself." That is all Eusebius knows of the supposed foundation of the see of St. Mark, and he does not seem to give it a high degree of confidence; it is clear that his sources were far from being as copious as he was accustomed to in some other settings.

There follows, in chapters 17–18 of the *Church History*, a long excursus concerning Philo's *On the Contemplative Life*, which Eusebius identifies as describing an early Christian community near Alexandria, ancestral to or at least foreshadowing the monastic milieus of his own time. This passage has given rise to extensive modern discussion that I cannot go into here. Then comes a more characteristic notice, in chapter 24: "In the eighth year of the reign of Nero Annianus was the first after Mark the evangelist to receive the *leitourgia* of the *paroikia* in Alexandria." Stephen Davis, in his recent book *The Early Coptic Papacy* (2004: 14–15), has summarized the scattered notices that follow in Eusebius about the succession to Mark and Annianus. None of them, for the period down to the late second century, betrays any actual information about any of the early bishops of Alexandria, other than their names and dates.

Alexandria did, of course, eventually develop a distinctively centralized episcopate leading a highly Christianized society with a vast network of local bishops. But Eusebius, as we have seen, had no real information about this developmental process before the episcopate of Demetrios (189–231), nor do we. There have been various reactions to this blank, including Attila Jakab's argument that there were no bishops of Alexandria before Demetrios, only a collection of presbyters.[7] This has become almost a counterorthodoxy, if we may judge by its adoption as a basic premise for understanding the position of Origen, in the new book of Anthony Grafton and Megan Williams (2006). But the logical consequences that might be derived from such a view, or from pre-Demetrian skepticism in general, for the development of the book in Egypt have hardly touched discussions of early Christian manuscripts actually known.[8]

It has been widely asserted, instead, or at least assumed, that the developments in the reign of Demetrios show that (and are understandable only on the assumption that) Christianity was widely disseminated in the Egyptian *chora* before this time, and that he in effect built on a substantial infrastructure, at least in the metropoleis of the nomes. This view has in large part been based on the existence of papyrus letters and manuscripts dated to the second century and coming from various provenances. This is true even in the work of so critical a historian as Ewa Wipszycka, who has rejected the Christian identity of some of what have been claimed to be the earliest private letters showing signs of Christianity.[9] This view, however, seems to me seriously open to question because of the insecure dating of the papyri. Perhaps equally problematic, it shows just how vital the existence and early dating of the papyri are to the entire conception of the development of Christianity in Egypt and how much is at stake in such datings. Without these early datings of papyri, we have no contemporary witnesses to pre-Demetrian Christianity to provide a background for his era.[10] It is worth the trouble at least to consider the consequences that would follow from taking a different view.

It may be helpful to summarize briefly some of the distinctive characteristics visible in the church of Egypt in late antiquity, as Wipszycka has outlined them. The episcopal network of Egypt developed relatively late in comparison with other regions; there were no metropolitan bishops in charge of subdivisions of the Egyptian province (which included Cyrenaica); the patriarch therefore had a direct relationship to all his bishops. Similarly within dioceses, priests had a direct relationship to their bishops. These characteristics were highly consequential for the history of the Egyptian church. What today in the language of management we might call an extremely flat structure, with a lack of intermediate layers of hierarchy, is very striking. Such structures have, as Wipszycka notes, various trade-offs of advantages and disadvantages. The chief executive, the bishop of Alexandria, had a relatively weak ability to watch over so many people carefully and adequately, thus allowing room for quite a bit of local freedom of maneuver. On the other hand, potential rivals to episcopal power were kept far from any position in which they could build up a substantial power base.

It would be surprising if a flat, monarchic structure of this kind had been universally popular. In fact there are many signs that the authoritarian ambitions of the see of Alexandria were not supported by everyone. Origen's need to leave Alexandria, late in Demetrios's reign, was probably a matter of a struggle over episcopal control of the teaching function, which was most likely not very institutionalized until that point (Jakab 2001: 169–73 and 216–27). The Meletian schism in the fourth century was mainly a question of the primacy of Alexandria over other bishops. Although Arius's clash with successive bishops is depicted by Athanasius throughout his works as a matter of false versus correct doctrine, something he could not claim about the Meletians, it seems that the Arian controversy was perennially insoluble precisely because it was *not* a matter of doctrinal agreement but of the struggle of the bishop to control a presbyter in his diocese and of widespread resistance to that type of control over preaching.

In the face of such a picture, it is hard not to adopt the extreme skeptic's position and wonder if the entire history of the see of Alexandria during its first century and a half, with its long but thin foundation story, was not part of an attempt, at the earliest in the time of Demetrios but perhaps not until a century or so later,[11] to create a legitimation by apostolicity for an otherwise contested monarchic power in the hands of the bishop.[12] Wipszycka, although not going so far as to see in Demetrios the first bishop of Alexandria, has proposed that we should see in Demetrios the originator of the network of bishops in the countryside, with only *presbyteroi* in place before him. She believes that he deliberately set out to episcopalize the *chora*, in the face of opposition from the *presbyteroi*. This may be correct, but it is worth observing that even so he consecrated, as far as we know, only three of them, which does not support the view that the much larger network we find at the end of the third century was really his creation.

But whether the larger network of bishops was the product of Demetrios or of his successor Heraklas, who was in office from 231 to 247 and consecrated twenty bishops to Demetrios's three, and in less than half the time that Demetrios had, it remains clear that at a minimum down to at least the end of the second century, and perhaps to the second quarter of the third, bishops did not exist outside Alexandria as they did in other Roman provinces. Why would this have been the case? Explanations seem of necessity to run in the direction of either a lack of desire on the part of the bishops in Alexandria to create such a body of local bishops or else their inability to do so. As I have indicated, Wipszycka thinks that the latter was the case, and this inability stemmed from opposition among the provincial clergy. But in part that view stems from the conviction that Christianity was indeed widespread in the countryside. Again, it is worth asking if this assumption might be wrong. What would be the consequences of imagining that in fact there were not very many Christians in the nomes?[13] That does not, of course, mean that we must go as far as Jakab, who has argued that there was essentially no evangelization of the *chora* before Heraklas,[14] just that we would not imagine that the numbers of Christians were very substantial.

Here we are brought back inescapably to the papyri, with a stronger sense of just how much stands or falls on our assessment of the value of the papyri, both documentary and literary, for second-century Egyptian Christianity. Documentary papyrology is in fact not of much help for the period before 300. The Roman government did not record religious affiliation in its census operations and indeed would have had no concept of "religion" in the modern sense at this period even if it thought it something worth asking people to declare. It is not until the declarations of sacrifice under Decius (249–251) that we can legitimately begin to look to the bureaucracy for any idea that it might record compliance or noncompliance with the state religion. Official records do not even designate individuals by Christian clerical titles in this period, nor do individuals describe themselves as presbyters or deacons in legal documents of this era. That is not in all likelihood a matter of self-concealment, which was not necessary during most of the third century, but of a sheer lack of the notion that the clergy formed an occupational or civil category deserving mention of this sort. The Christian clergy was not thought of in the same category as, for example, the Egyptian priesthoods, access to which brought fiscal privileges and was therefore carefully controlled by the state. There are just a couple of instances, from the second half of the third century, when people are identified as "Christians," and these rarities occur in a fashion that makes it speculative how to interpret them.[15] AnneMarie Luijendijk's recent Harvard dissertation has suggested that "Christian" may in fact in some cases be a way of identifying someone as a member of the clergy, a professional Christian, so to speak (Luijendijk forthcoming). This is an attractive notion, but it does not widen the evidence very much. At all events, neither official records nor private contracts offer any hope of recovering second-century Christianity in Egypt.[16] That fact has long been understood, at least in a kind of general fashion, even if not really internalized.

In consequence, successive compilers of Christian letters have done their best to find private letters that could be dated before the Tetrarchy (293–305). The general difficulty of dating many letter-hands, particularly the less skilled, has made this a perilous enterprise. Much ingenuity has indeed been devoted to trying to identify such letters written in the second century, but with essentially no result.[17] Mario Naldini, although excessively given to describing epistolary banalities as fervent expressions of Christian faith,[18] recognized the problem. Following in the footsteps of Colin Roberts,[19] he admitted the scarcity of such letters but argued that one could nonetheless say with confidence that Christianity was widespread in the cities and towns of Egypt in the second century, because the biblical and related papyri had come from a wide range of provenances (Naldini 1968/1998: 34, 58). The earliest letter that can be said certainly to be written by a Christian, because of the use of a distinctively Christian abbreviated religious term, ἐν κ(υρί)ῳ, *P.Bas.* 16 (Naldini no. 4), is dated to the early third century, thus to the period of Demetrios's episcopate or at the latest that of his successor. There are a number of other such letters, securely Christian, datable to the latter part of the third century, and some reasonable assignments to the earlier part of the third century. But letters datable to the second century with confidence are never securely Christian, and letters with definite marks of Christianity are not firmly datable to the second century.

With official documents, private documents, and even private letters failing to yield the desired information, the critical importance of the literary papyri for a Christian presence in the Egyptian countryside in the second century is thus all the more obvious, as Naldini and Roberts already recognized. These are, in effect, the last hope of finding a pre-Demetrian Christianity outside Alexandria, whatever one may think about the usability of the later literary tradition for reconstructing the situation in Alexandria itself. A great deal of church history is dependent on them. If there was a significant body of biblical or other theological texts in circulation in places like Oxyrhynchus, Arsinoe, and Hermopolis in the second century, we will have to accept that the lack of other evidence is just a product of the ways in which people did not feel any reason to record their Christian identity in everyday written form. But if there is no such body of Christian manuscripts, we may be entitled to suspect, with Jakab, that the widespread presence of Christianity in the countryside before Demetrios is an illusion. If so, the long-standing baffled disappointment of papyrologists and those who follow papyrological work in the face of the relative silence of the documentary papyri would only be intensified. The level of this disappointment, however, is a result not only of the silence of the papyri taken on their own but also of the fact that I remarked on earlier, namely, that we also have so little other evidence for Christianity in the period before the episcopate of Demetrios and that hopes for the contribution of the papyri were correspondingly high. The period of Demetrios is of course rich in literary remains of the Alexandrian church, with the voluminous output of both Clement and Origen to give a sense of the lively and contentious intellectual atmosphere of this church in this period. But before Clement the picture is close to blank, just as with the papyrus documents and letters. And Grafton and Williams (2006) have argued forcefully that this literary work is to be seen in terms of normal ancient literary and philosophical work, based on independent means of the writer or of a patron, as in the case of Origen, and did not rely on ecclesiastical infrastructure; they date the creation of serious intellectual work in that kind of institutional framework only to the episcopacy of Eusebius in Caesarea.

There is one other point to be made about the consequences of failure to find evidence of second-century Christianity. The conclusion that Christianity was pretty much limited to Alexandria (with its large Jewish community, devastated under Trajan) and other places from which we have no papyri has not been the only possible explanation offered for the general lack of evidence. There has also been Walter Bauer's thesis that Egypt's Christianity was heterodox and therefore effectively concealed from view by a posterity that rejected that kind of Christianity.[20] In fact, however, heterodoxy does not really fare any better than orthodoxy—(these are, I know, problematic and retrospective terms, but that does not need to concern us in the present context)—in this assessment, because there is little sign of the Gnostics (who are usually the group mainly in view—this is of course another problematic term) in the second-century papyri either. If the absence of papyrus witnesses other than the uncertainly dated biblical papyri is a sign that orthodox Christianity was missing, it is just as good a witness for the absence of Gnosticism.[21]

When we look to the possibility that the manuscripts will rescue us from this deep pit of ignorance, we must confront at the start the basic difficulty of dating manuscripts written in the ancient world, because of the absence, in most cases, of external evidence for the date and because of the approximateness and subjectivity of dates based on the styles of handwriting used in these manuscripts. Book-hands aspire to regularity, and their style changes only slowly over the decades. They are far harder to date accurately than are the hands of documentary papyri, and minor variations or individual letter-forms are rarely reliable guides. In the case of the biblical papyri commonly assigned to the second century, with which I shall be concerned here, everything rests on such fallible palaeographical dating. I am using the term "biblical" here in a broad sense, to include noncanonical works as well as the Old Testament and New Testament canons, but that does not actually change the situation significantly in this case.

Let us turn, then, to look at the papyri bearing biblical texts and given relatively early dates by some of the scholars who have studied them, leaving aside for the moment the controversy of a decade ago over some supposed first-century gospel fragments and also the earliest fragments of the *Shepherd* of Hermas, both of which require an extended discussion of their own (chapter 2). These papyri with early dates bear the burden not only of helping to indicate whether there were Christians in the Egyptian hinterland (and what sorts of Christians they were) but also of telling us whether the Christians were leaders in the use of the codex (chapter 4)—heavy burdens indeed for what are mostly small scraps.

I shall take as a starting point the dates given for texts in the Leuven Database of Ancient Books,[22] which does not represent any particular school of thought on this point. That eclecticism is not free of problems, but it will at least avoid any particular structural bias at the beginning. We find there one Christian codex fragment assigned a date to the late first or early second century, and six more dated to the second century. Apparent pride of place goes to a fragment of Psalms published four decades ago by J.W.B. Barns and G. D. Kilpatrick.[23] They do not in fact date this papyrus to the turn of the century, as the Leuven Database seems to suggest, but rather state that it "is more likely to be the second century A.D. than the third," a view that is restated a page later in their article as, "the papyrus may belong anywhere from the end of the first century to the end of the second." In other words, they assign it to the second century. They compare its handwriting to that of two other early biblical papyri, *P.Ant.* I 7 and *P.Ryl.* III 457, of which the first is another fragment of Psalms, the latter a New Testament fragment to which we shall come shortly. Like *P.Ant.* I 7,[24] the text published by Barns and Kilpatrick presents no distinctively Christian characteristics except, arguably, the use of the codex format. In both cases, then, there is some risk of circular argument in identifying the texts as Christian rather than Jewish. (On this question, see below, p. 24.) The editor of the Antinoopolis papyrus dated it to the middle of the second century.

In both of these cases of Psalms fragments, the most thorough study of the history of the early codices, by Sir Eric Turner (1977), offers a later date, namely, second to third century. That, as it happens, is also the date assigned in the Bodleian's register for the Psalms fragment, quite likely deriving from the opinion of Arthur Hunt, whose widow donated it to the Bodleian. Grenfell and Hunt are regularly described in much of the more recent scholarly literature about the codex as having assigned excessively late dates to many of their finds, as a result of an a priori judgment that codex fragments should not be found before the fourth century.[25] That may have been true in the early stages of their work, but it is not necessarily a fair assumption about their later work, when the finds from Oxyrhynchus had made it clear that codices occurred in the third century. Indeed, the Hunt who would have dated the Psalms fragment to the end of the second or the beginning of the third century obviously did not think that codices started in the fourth century![26] As we shall see, Turner, who knew vastly more early codices than Grenfell and Hunt or indeed practically anyone else before or afterward, fairly consistently also opted for later dates than those that the editors of papyri and other commentators had offered.

The third of the fragments assigned an early date, *P.Bad.* IV 56 (figure 1.1), also contains a work from the Jewish scriptures, this time of Exodus. It was found at Qarara, ancient Hipponon in the Herakleopolite nome, and dated to the second century by its editor, Friedrich Bilabel, without offering any parallels or analysis. It contains *nomina sacra* written in the Christian fashion and is thus more definitely a Christian production than either of the Psalms fragments. Turner assigned it to the late second century.[27]

Turning now to the canonical gospels, there are again three fragments attributed to the second century. The first of these is a small bit of the Gospel of John in the John Rylands Library in Manchester, of unknown provenance.[28] It is the only fragment dated by Turner to the second century without qualification. More recently, however, one scholar has argued that it should be reassigned to the early third century, on the basis of a comparison with *P.Chester Beatty* X.[29] That may be too definitive, but an exhaustive article by Brent Nongbi (2005) has brought forward a range of palaeographical parallels that undermine confidence in an early date, even if they do not fully establish one in the late second or early third century.

The second New Testament fragment, *P.Oxy.* L 3523, also of John (figure 1.2), was assigned to the second century by T. C. Skeat, its first editor. He offered as palaeographic parallels P.Egerton 2, which is more generally dated to the turn of the second to third centuries, and *P.Oxy.* IV 656, which he and Bell assigned to the second century but which Turner (Old Testament 9) again dated II/III.

Figure 1.1. *P.Bad.* IV 56. Photo courtesy of Institut für Papyrologie, University of Heidelberg.

The third gospel fragment, from Matthew (figure 1.3), was recently published as *P.Oxy.* LXIV 4404 by David Thomas (LDAB 2935). The editor noted its similarity to the fragment of John that I have just discussed and proposed a date in the later second century.

Finally, there is one apocryphal gospel (figure 1.4), as it was identified by its editors, Peter Parsons and Dieter Lührmann, *P.Oxy.* LX 4009 (LDAB 4872). They supposed it to be of the second rather than the third century, and the nonliterary parallels they offer, although not terribly close, seem to belong more to the early and middle parts of the century than to its latter part.

Apart from this last item, what is striking to me about this group of papyri is that there is not much disagreement among those who have studied them about what papyri they may legitimately be compared

FIGURE 1.2. *P.Oxy.* L 3523. Photo courtesy of the Egypt Exploration Society.

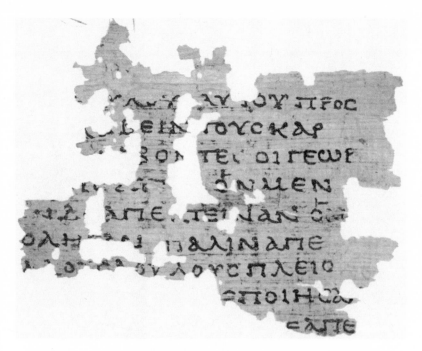

Figure 1.3. *P.Oxy.* LXIV 4404. Photo courtesy of the Egypt Exploration Society.

to. There are comparisons within the group, and there are comparisons to several papyri generally dated to the end of the second or beginning of the third century. Disagreement arises only about where the entire cluster should be dated. One may see one camp, typically consisting, across the generations, of Bell, Roberts, and Skeat, which prefers an early date for the group, and another, represented in more recent times by Turner and Thomas, but originally by Grenfell and Hunt, arguing that the entire cluster should be put later. There is on average perhaps a half century or a bit more between the positions of these two camps. Herbert Hunger has also argued for the earlier date, seemingly happier to push them back to the very start of the second century or the end of the first than to have them dated later (Hunger 1960: esp. 20). Only the fragmentary apocryphal gospel stands outside this discussion, detached from the relatively enclosed circle of palaeographic parallels adduced.

Figure 1.4. *P.Oxy.* LX 4009. Photo courtesy of the Egypt Exploration Society.

The number of papyri dated to the general zone of the late second to early third century, or, even more vaguely, of the second to third century, is much larger. The Leuven Database includes—apart from the items already mentioned—some twenty papyri in that range. If six out of the "second-century seven" already discussed were added to that, we would have twenty-six papyri dated to this period, compared with only one before the late second century. Obviously these two views can have enormously different consequences for our conclusions about the diffusion of Christianity in the second century.

It is interesting, I think, to look at the breakdown of these relatively early texts by the works represented (table 1.1). At this point, it is useful, even necessary, to look more deeply into the assumptions underlying all these scholarly agonizings about the numbers of Christian papyri in the second and third centuries. We might well

Table 1.1
Christian Papyri Dated to the Second and/or Early Third Centuries

	Dated II or II/III	Dated early III	Total
Old Testament	3	8	11
New Testament	3	6	9
New Testament Apocrypha	1	2	3
Hermas	1	3	4
Dubiously Christian	0	2	2
Total	8	21	29

ask how many we should expect to find—in comparison with *what standard* are we thinking that there are few or many?

Obviously our surviving papyri come from a small minority of the ancient communities of Egypt, and even among these only a tiny fraction of all that were written have survived; an even smaller percentage have been edited. Peter van Minnen has estimated that published papyri amount to somewhere between one-twelfth and one-twentieth of his guess at a total of known numbers of papyri in all collections, an estimate that is in the range of 1 million to 1.5 million, and there is little information publicly available on what the unpublished material consists of (Van Minnen 2009). In any event, probably the most we might hope to have in the published papyri would be for the number of Christian literary papyri, set against the total of literary texts, to be proportionate to the Christians' share of the population at a given moment.

There are, to be sure, reasons both why this estimate might be too optimistic and why it might be too pessimistic. Christian books not only did not in this period have the advantage of being part of the educational system—the reason why we have so much Homer in the papyri, for example—but also should have suffered from the systematic destruction of Christian books ordered during some of the later persecutions. There are other elements also affecting the Christian share of published literary texts. First, editors have been more eager to edit Christian fragments than any other, precisely because of the intense interest generated by such texts and the issues at stake in dating them.[30] Second, some of the fragments might be dated too early for the same reason. The second of these points is of course at the focus of our inquiry. As to the first, I do not know how to quantify it. Every papyrologist will instinctively consider it likely to be true. New Testament fragments sell for far more than comparable papyri of other types, and they generate more visits to papyrus collections and their Web sites than any other type of papyrus. No one who identified an early fragment of a Christian text in a papyrus collection would be likely to leave it unpublished.

For the sake of the following argument, I shall assume that the various crosscurrents I have described cancel one another. That is, I shall assume that the lower probability of original creation and of ancient survival of Christian texts is negated, but not outweighed, by the much higher modern probability of publication of those pieces that do survive. It is most unlikely that this assumption is exactly right, of course. If anything it will be mistaken in the direction of overstating the likely proportion of Christian texts, above all because the influence of classical *paideia* undoubtedly increased the volume of Homer papyri, perhaps overbalancing the likelihood that most collections have been scoured for Christian texts. In the final chapter, I shall also explore the possible implications for this question of the economics of book production.

We would then want to ask what proportion of the population was Christian and likely to possess Christian books. We do not, of course, have accurate figures about the percentage of the population that was Christian in the second and third centuries, nor will we ever have them. The census did not, as I already remarked, record such information, and in fact no one ever knew what the figures were. But models of what these numbers might have been have been offered by Keith Hopkins and Rodney Stark (Hopkins 1998; Stark 1996: esp. 3–27); as for our purposes these do not differ significantly and they use similar methodologies, I shall use here Stark's calculation that the rate of growth of the Christian population ought to have been somewhere in the neighborhood of 3.4 percent per year (or 40 percent per decade). He bases this estimate on the twin assumptions that

Christians numbered only a thousand in the whole empire in 40 CE and that they were an overwhelming majority by the late fourth century. Both of these points are controversial, but neither is likely to be wrong by enough to alter the results where they matter for our present purposes. It should be stressed, indeed, that different assumptions, particularly about the dominance of Christianity in the late fourth century, would be much more likely to strengthen the point I am going to make than to weaken it.

A more serious objection might be that the growth rate is not likely to have been constant; but if this objection is correct, as I think it surely is, then Stark's assumption of a constant growth rate will flatter the number of Christians in the earlier period. The reason is simple: the most likely shape for the curve of the rate of Christianization, that is, the rate of growth of the Christian population as a percentage of the entire population, if it was not a straight line, is the S-shaped curve of the logistic function, which has been widely observed in phenomena of diffusion ranging from religious conversion to technology change. That means that the growth rate in the earlier centuries and at the end of the period was probably slower and the rate in the middle—from the mid-third to the mid-fourth century, probably—was steeper.

I now present a table embodying Stark's simpler assumptions about growth, which will, as I have indicated, have if anything a tendency to exaggerate the number of Christians in the second century (table 1.2). It is based on the assumption that Egypt amounted to about a tenth of the population of the empire, for which I am using the conventional figure of 55 million. The argument about percentages will not, however, be affected if one prefers a different total, and those scholars who believe that the number was higher would also put the population of Egypt higher as well.

According to these estimates, Christians did not amount to as much as 1 percent of the population until the late 220s—near the end of Demetrios's episcopate, in other words. I stress again that even though none of these figures is likely to be correct, their approximate level would not be affected very much by almost any plausible changes that one might make in the assumptions.

So when Demetrios came to the episcopal throne in Alexandria, there were probably fewer than twenty thousand Christians in all

TABLE 1.2
Estimated Size of Christian Population in Egypt

Date	Number of Christians	Percent of population
100	753	0.014
125	1,746	0.032
150	4,047	0.074
175	9,382	0.170
200	21,747	0.395
225	50,409	0.917
250	116,849	2.120

of Egypt. I suggest now that we look at the total numbers of literary papyri—fragments of books of all types—for three chronological slices, the first to second century, the second century, and the second to third century,[31] set against the expected or probable number of Christian texts that would be proportionate to their share of the population (table 1.3). I have obtained the expected number of Christian books (column 3 in the table) by multiplying the average of the beginning, middle, and ending percentages of Christians in the population (column 2) times the total number of known "books" (column 1), using the broad Leuven definition of books, about which I shall say a little more later on.[32]

TABLE 1.3
Expected Number of Surviving Christian Books

Period	Book fragments	Christian percentage of population	Probable Christian books
I/II	403	0.014	0.056
II	1,474	0.092	1.360
II/III	813	1.482	12.000

There is, to judge by the figures in this table, only one chance in eighteen that *any* Christian book of the late first or early second century would survive. That is, the odds are seventeen to one that we would have zero such books. We should have just one or two Christian fragments from the second century as a whole. On any reckoning, the number of published fragments of Christian character usually assigned to these early periods considerably exceeds the expected number. At all events, there are no grounds for thinking that we have a small number of Christian papyri compared with the likely proportion of Christians in the population, let alone Gnostics. The reverse is true. It is time to let go of the idea that Christian literature is somehow underrepresented in the papyri before the later third century. If the early dates attributed to Christian texts are accepted, they are actually grossly overrepresented. If the later dates are taken to be correct, the second century has about the right number—one, most likely—and the turn of the century is significantly oversupplied with Christian books. At all events, the basic congruity between what exists and what the model predicts is interesting and encouraging.

It is impossible to leave this point, however, without trying to assess a little further the initial likelihood of the existence of Christian books. Why would someone make a copy of one of the gospels or epistles, or of a collection of them? And how does the motivation and likelihood of such book production compare with that of classical literature? I have already mentioned one important factor, the role of the standard classical education of the elite of Graeco-Roman Egypt (Cribiore 2001). Many of the ancient "books" included in the Leuven Database are not books at all but only excerpts from them that served the purpose of pedagogy. The literature that individuals possessed at home as adults also reflected the authors they had read in school. By contrast, we have little evidence for the private lay ownership of biblical texts at any early date, and even later, ownership of Christian books by individuals may not have been extensive. Even in Constantinople and with an affluent body of worshippers, John Chrysostom did not expect many to have, let alone to read, the scriptures at home (MacMullen 1989).

An obvious point of critical interest is the clergy, who were both the persons likely to acquire scriptures for their churches and the individuals most likely to need biblical texts for their own use.

Remarkably little is known about most of the Egyptian clergy as individuals. Wipszycka ascribes their main source of recruitment to the "middle classes" but without defining that term (something that is of course extremely difficult), and she goes on to speak of their need for a good education (Wipszycka 2007a). A good education, however, suggests family wealth with which to pay for the education, even if not necessarily membership in the very top stratum of society. Despite examples like Synesius of Cyrene, there is not much to suggest that the highest-ranking aristocrats were recruited for the clergy, even as bishops, although this may have changed over time. Quite possibly some bishops came, like Augustine, from the curial class. As with so much else in the clergy, much would have varied according to the wealth and importance of the see.

The recruitment of *presbyteroi* and deacons is also very poorly known, but it is now better understood than it was in the past because of the recent studies of Egypt by Georg Schmelz and of Asia Minor by Sabine Hübner (Schmelz 2002; Hübner 2005). For small-town south Asia Minor, Hübner shows that presbyters and deacons came heavily from a stratum that can be defined as middle-class in a local sense, that is, against the background of the communities. They were in many cases the kin of merchants and craftsmen of substance. No doubt there were also many small to medium landowners, as the appearances of clergy in Egyptian land registers suggest. Overall, there is every reason to expect a correlation between an individual's initial social status and his clerical position. A matching of that sort would fit well with the differential needs of education at the various levels, urban and rural.

The increased monastic recruitment of bishops and even other clergy in later periods may not have changed this situation much. Monasticism was, as is by now well established, not a uniform movement in social terms but also reflected a wide range of origins and statuses. In any case, because the clergy in Egypt had no formal training and the church had no institutions for providing such a professional education, there was no way to avoid a reasonably close match between their status of origin, and thus their education, and their rank in the clergy; monasticism may have helped a bit to level gaps in formation.

Perhaps the best conclusion we can draw from all these considerations is that the *presbyteroi* of the Egyptian church in the third and
fourth centuries are likely to have come from an approximately rep-
resentative sample of the classes who received a grammarian-level education in the metropoleis of the nomes in this period. How many of
them there might have been is hard to say. To extend speculation just
a bit further, let us imagine that of our twenty thousand hypothetical
Christians in Egypt at the beginning of the episcopate of Demetrios,
a quarter were in Alexandria. That might be a low estimate for the
degree of concentration in the capital. But even such a low figure for
Alexandria would leave just fifteen thousand in the nomes, or something like three hundred per nome. It is hard to see why the average
nome would have needed a clergyman of higher status than presbyter,
and the absence of bishops at this time seems in this light not terribly
significant. If we suppose, as I think likely, that the majority of these
Christians were in the metropoleis, we need not suppose the existence
of village *presbyteroi*. It is hard to imagine that more than a hundred
Christian clergy of a rank requiring a grammarian's education existed
in all of Egypt, and the number may have been substantially lower.
Their proportionate share of educated adults is in any case unlikely
to have exceeded their share of the population as a whole, somewhere
shy of 0.4 percent.[33] Altogether, however, this should lead us to the
conclusion that there is no reason to suppose that Christians were
disproportionately more likely than other people to own books.

My conclusion is not a negative one in the sense that I would argue that there were not Christians in second-century Egypt. Instead,
it seems to me that their numbers and structure were such that we
should recognize frankly that it would be only a lucky coincidence
if we were to find a Christian text, be it letter or manuscript, from
the period before Demetrios—before the Severan period, to put
it in Roman political terms. To accept this view means, of course,
admitting a kind of defeat. We cannot expect the papyri to save us
from our ignorance of the nature and development of the Egyptian
church in the pre-Severan period. That is undoubtedly not going to
be welcome news for many people. But it is in my eyes the only realistic assessment of the probabilities, and it has the virtue that it frees
us from the struggle to push the dates of manuscripts back into the

second century, or even into the first. Instead, the natural sense of palaeographical comparisons can be followed without an unreasonable zeal for finding origins. This strikes me as a welcome liberation, which papyrologists should embrace, because it is only with the preoccupation with origins set aside that the interest and original contribution of the few genuinely early texts can be assessed properly.

Earlier in this chapter (p. 11) I remarked on the potential for circular reasoning in distinguishing Christian from Jewish books when dealing with texts of the Jewish scriptures, the Christian Old Testament. In one sense, any identifications of early codex fragments as Jewish rather than Christian would only strengthen the larger argument made here that there is far less evidence for Christian books before the late second century than usually claimed. The difficulties posed by the use of abbreviated sacred vocabulary (the "nomina sacra") and the codex form in distinguishing Christian from Jewish books have generated a long discussion, for which Kurt Treu's analysis (1973/1991: excursus) is fundamental. The most recent thorough discussion (Choat 2006: 119–25) concludes that, with the exception of Manichaean texts, "no instance of a *nomen sacrum* in an unquestionably non-Christian documentary text on papyrus is known to me." It is obviously impossible to prove that such an instance could not occur, but that impossibility provides no support for any positive argument in favor of non-Christian use. I shall therefore take it as a given that the *nomina sacra* in texts written before the diffusion of Manichaeism are signs of Christianity.

The situation with the codex differs in that there are more cases in which it is impossible to make a clear distinction between Christian and Jewish origin. In some of these (Genesis and Psalms dominate the material) there are characteristics that have seemed to Treu (1973/1991) and others to make Jewish provenance more likely, although they could also be signs of the continuing presence of strongly Jewish traits in early Christianity. The argument is complicated by the near-total absence of documentary evidence for a Jewish population in Egypt between the revolt that ended at the start of Hadrian's reign (117) and the late third century. In any event, as will become apparent in chapter 4, if a few of the codices sometimes identified as Christian were in fact of Jewish origin, the argument presented there about the diffusion of the codex would only be strengthened.

Two Case Studies

In the previous chapter I described in general terms the forces, both academic and religious, that have made the study and particularly the palaeographic dating of early Christian books in Egypt such a difficult and even distorted subject. I suggested that a realistic assessment of the probable size and character of the Christian communities in Egypt in the second century of our era would lead us to see how unlikely it is that we would possess more than one or two pieces of Christian text from any time before the Severan period (193–235), when Demetrios was bishop of Alexandria and the construction of a network of bishops outside Alexandria, in the nome capitals, had its first, hesitant beginnings.

In this chapter I shall examine in more detail two specific, controversial cases of the dating of fragmentary manuscripts that I left aside in chapter 1. One of them concerns long-known material and a controversy of roughly a decade ago about what were the earliest fragments of the gospels known on papyrus; the other involves a volume of *Oxyrhynchus Papyri* published in 2005, in which three new papyrus manuscripts of the *Shepherd* of Hermas were published by Nikolaos Gonis. Both of these cases are instructive about different aspects of the general problem that I have been trying to sketch.

Readers may find it entirely excessive that I should devote much of a chapter to the ten-year-old affair of the late Carsten Peter Thiede, his article in *ZPE*, and the book that followed it. I do not think that many papyrologists gave any credence at the time to his attempt to redate several papyri to the first century. But as far as I know, no full analysis of Thiede's claims has ever been presented, certainly not in any form that would reach a broad scholarly public.[1] Moreover, as an episode in the sociology of scholarship it is of exceptional interest, and it helps to illuminate the entire range of pressures that have propelled the study of early manuscripts by providing an extreme example—a kind of boundary case that helps us see what lies further from the boundaries as well. We shall see even more acutely why the general subject that I have chosen is not something of purely academic interest and why alertness to agendas, stated and unstated, is essential. This is, of course, true with almost anything to do with the study of Judaism and Christianity, and perhaps with the study of religion more generally. Even the most gruesome details of this episode have some interest in sensitizing us to issues that come up in other places and forms. I must say that I also found it at the time, and find it still, a useful experience to bear in mind in thinking about the interaction of scholarship with the popular media and in considering broader issues of subjectivity or objectivity and the personal note in scholarship. If it is a somewhat horrifying object lesson, it is nonetheless a valuable one.

I may also mention my own experience in dealing with this controversy, which taught me how high the stakes are to many people. A Lutheran newsletter of opinion published an editor's note praising the book of Thiede and D'Ancona that I shall be discussing. I wrote to the editor saying that I thought this praise was not warranted. My note was published, and in the following issue was a letter from a theology professor at a conservative seminary denouncing me as antievangelical for saying that Thiede's book was not respectable as papyrological scholarship. It would probably not be worth saying that I do not actually have any personal stake in most of the conclusions of twentieth-century biblical scholarship or in a late date for the gospels. Neither an early nor a later date would have any religious significance for me.

Thiede was, I think it is fair to say, not a well-known figure to papyrologists at the time that he burst into public prominence. As far as I can determine, he had no papyrological training or experience, and his professional position did not concern papyrology (he was director of the Institut für Wissenschaftstheoretische Grundlagenforschung in Paderborn).[2] He had, however, played a certain role in earlier discussions of a Qumran papyrus, the controversial 7Q5, and to anyone paying attention at that time—which I certainly was not—the main traits found in his later publications would already have been visible. Thiede had sided with those accepting Jose O'Callaghan's identification of this papyrus as a fragment from the Gospel of Mark.[3] Qumran, of course, has its own rich and complex scholarly and public history, which I do not intend to discuss here, and which has unfolded largely separate from the course of papyrology.

It was the publication of Thiede's article "Papyrus Magdalen Greek 17 (Gregory-Aland P64). A Reappraisal," in *Zeitschrift für Papyrologie und Epigraphik* 105, in 1995, that brought him more generally to the notice of papyrologists, simply because of the prominence of the journal in which the article was published. This article was written in a classically "objective" style, with normal academic turgidity and an apparent absence of personal agenda. All the conclusions were carefully hedged, even if their potential impact was revolutionary. That does not mean that the arguments themselves followed accepted scholarly procedures, but they attempted to give the impression of doing so.

The article had in fact been preceded by extensive press coverage the previous Christmas, in which the main lines of the argument of the article were put before the public. The fullest version of this that I have seen is in the *Times* (of London) on December 23, 1994.

Thiede argued in the article that the Magdalen papyrus, along with other parts of the same manuscript then in Barcelona, was to be dated to the first century. In his more public statements, like the *Times* coverage at Christmas 1994, he pushed the date back still further, and the book published the following year by Thiede and his journalist coauthor, Matthew D'Ancona, adopted the same approach as the public statements. In the book, Thiede is always spoken of in the third person and cited almost as if he were some outside authority, rather than being an insider, one of the arguers of the case in the book. Despite the frequent reference later in the book to the article as the foundation and demonstration of the technical case for an early date, in fact the public and scholarly sides of Thiede's case diverged almost from the outset, a divergence that he did not generally acknowledge in either forum.

This divergence, this option to present the case to a broad public with one date, to the scholarly community with a different date, but to treat the more public case (and its consequences) as having been demonstrated by the scholarly publication, makes it difficult to frame an analysis of the case in a coherent fashion. The two presentations are different, and their arguments need to be followed in different paths; at the same time, they maintain a kind of relationship and in effect ask the reader to treat them as interdependent. I must confess that I find it hard to escape the thought that this approach was taken precisely to baffle would-be challengers.

Anyone who has had much dealing with the press will be aware that the relationship between what is said to a reporter and what appears in print is often at least indirect, if not altogether difficult to find. For this reason, I shall leave aside the press coverage of Thiede's initial announcement of what he persistently described as a discovery, and begin with the ostensibly, even ostentatiously scholarly article in *ZPE*, then turn to the book.

The article does not announce itself as concerned primarily with the date of the Matthew fragments, and indeed in the book (p. 2) it was later claimed that the reexamination of the Magdalen papyrus (figure 2.1) was "a routine act of scholarly curiosity." This statement is contradicted in the book itself, but the article starts out with some attempts to establish Thiede's bona fides as a scholar, by announcing that the inventory number of the papyrus was not quite what had always been said, and by suggesting some slightly different readings from those of the first editor, C. H. Roberts (what Wachtel was later to describe ironically as "eine nicht ganz unerhebliche Verbesserung des Transkripts"). Thiede notes that the Oxford and (then) Barcelona fragments (figure 2.2), belonging to the same codex (P64+67 in the usual numbering of New Testament papyrus manuscripts), represented the earliest known manuscript of Matthew, but he rejects the possibility that the fragments of Luke in the Bibliothèque nationale de France in Paris (P4), which he proposes to date up to a century later, come from the same multigospel codex as the Matthew fragments. We shall return to that question later.

Figure 2.1. Magdalen papyrus Ms. Gr. 17. Photo courtesy the President and Fellows of Magdalen College Oxford.

Thiede's discussion of the date opens with a recapitulation of dates proposed by earlier scholars: the third century as suggested by the original purchaser, Charles Huleatt, who had no particular qualifications in the matter; the preference for the fourth century on the part of Arthur Hunt; the consensus of British papyrology—Sir Harold Bell, Colin Roberts, Theodore Skeat, and Sir Eric Turner—for a date at the end of the second century (ca. 200). Thiede then offers (p. 15) his manifesto for a reexamination:

> Since the publication of Roberts' paper, new papyri have become available, and they appear to favour an even earlier date. This may not come as a surprise, since one tendency of the reevaluation of NT papyri at least since the 60s has been a redating with, occasionally, somewhat drastic and not undisputed consequences. It may be argued that the result of this continuing process is a mounting degree of uncertainty, rather than certainty, as to the reliability of palaeographical datings of literary hands; but even so, one should not eschew the challenge.

Figure 2.2. Fragment of Matthew, P.Monts. Roca 1. Photo courtesy Abadia de Montserrat.

The footnote to this passage offers two examples of such reexaminations, in which arguments were made for the redating of *P.Bodmer* II and *P.Chester Beatty* II to the beginning of the second century (Hunger 1960; Kim 1988). No information is offered about the bases for these redatings or their relevance to the Matthew fragments.

Instead, Thiede proceeds to offer what he thinks is an attractive parallel to the Matthew fragments. Parenthetically, it should be said that the fragments (P67) now in the Abbey of Montserrat are ignored almost throughout Thiede's discussion, which focuses only on the Magdalen fragments. No good reason for this silence is ever visible. The parallel adduced is a Minor Prophets leather roll (figure 2.3) found at Naḥal Ḥever (8HevXIIgr), for which he cites a range of proposed dates stretching from the late first century BCE to the later first century CE. After picking out several letters in which he sees similarities, Thiede proceeds:

Figure 2.3. 8HevXIIgr. Photo courtesy of the Israel Antiquities Authority.

The Naḥal Ḥever scroll of the Minor Prophets may be at the extreme end of the spectrum, but is not the only first century analogy. Further material is provided by papyri in the script of Herculaneum, for which 79 CE is the natural focal point. Interestingly, there is a small, unidentified Greek fragment from Qumran Cave 7, 7Q61, for which the archaeological *terminus ante quem* is 68 CE, which has the characteristic *Eta* with the horizontal stroke above the median, evident in Magdalen Gr. 17. There also is a Greek papyrus from Qumran Cave 4 which shows several letters resembling Papyrus Magdalen Gr. 17, such as the *Alpha*, the *Beta*, etc.: pap4QLXXLeviticus[b]. As Parsons points out, the script is far from uniform, but this papyrus from Cave 4 could be dated to the mid-first century AD.

The reference here to Herculaneum, which is mentioned only in passing, is remarkable. Thiede offers no citation of specific texts or palaeographical features as having similarities to the Matthew codex—this is all just a drive-by shooting, in effect, invoking the single most famous closed archaeological context with a precise date. But even if one were to agree that there were similarities between the Matthew papyrus and the Herculaneum papyri, this would not in fact give much comfort to a date in the middle to later first century CE. The books of Herculaneum almost certainly for the most part derive from the library of the philosopher Philodemus himself, who died about a century and a quarter before the eruption of Vesuvius.[4] An argument relying on such similarity would therefore support putting this manuscript of Matthew at a date before the birth of Jesus. That would be revolutionary, but I do not think it would have much chance of being right.

Thiede wraps up his palaeographic comparison of the Matthew papyrus with the material from Naḥal Ḥever, Qumran, and Herculaneum in these words (p. 17):

> But, and this is the point, the prevailing tendency to date material of a nature comparable to Magdalen Gr. 17 to a period even preceding the earliest possible date of Matthew's gospel suggests, with all due caution, the possibility of redating the fragments from Oxford and Barcelona—which are, after all, definitely Matthean—to a period somewhat earlier than the late second century previously assigned to them. Certainty will remain elusive, of course.

The argument proceeds, after a brief and inconclusive nod in the direction of *nomina sacra*, to the question of the possibility that a text in the form of a codex could have been created before 100 CE. He quotes Roberts and Skeat as favoring the likelihood that Christians adopted the codex before that date, asserting that the Magdalen/Montserrat papyrus may provide the specific, concrete evidence for this otherwise hypothetical possibility as a "prime example" of this early use of the codex. From this, he arrives at his main conclusion: "it may be argued that it [the Matthew codex] could be redated from the late second to the late first century, some time after the destruction of the Temple in Jerusalem" (19).

The article thus chose as palaeographical comparanda only texts with an archaeological or historical *terminus ante quem*; it cited as authorities works supporting the position being argued but without examining their evidence or reasons; and its palaeographical arguments were based almost entirely on similarities of specific letter shapes, rather than the overall character of handwritings.

The reaction from biblical papyrology was not long delayed. Just two volumes later in the same journal, in the same year, appeared an article by Klaus Wachtel, from the Institut für Neutestamentliche Textforschung in Münster (Wachtel 1996). Thiede refers to this article in his book with some hostility—not surprising, because Hans-Udo Rosenbaum of the same institute had crossed swords with him over Qumran in the previous decade.[5] In the article Wachtel rejects the supposed similarities with the Naḥal Ḥever and Qumran texts in some detail, arguing that they belong to wholly different types of handwriting. (When I showed the images of the Naḥal Ḥever Minor Prophets and the Matthew codex to graduate students with almost no experience of papyrology, even they could see at once what Wachtel demonstrates at length.) The detailed demolition of the Minor Prophets comparison in Wachtel's article perhaps explains Thiede's more pronounced use, in the book, of Herculaneum and other texts as his comparanda. More broadly, Wachtel points out from the start, alluding to the more dramatic claims in the London press, "Von einem Augenzeugenbericht über das Leben Christi ist hier freilich nicht mehr die Rede." He points out also that the *nomina sacra*, which Thiede adduced as a supplementary argument for an early date, are of no significance for that question, as they are found in Christian manuscripts of all dates. As he puts it, if the first-century date were correct, then of course the papyrus would be an example of *nomina sacra* and the codex at that period. But that's a large, even insurmountable, "if."

To return to the question of the Paris fragments of Luke, P4: In the article, Thiede voices the opinion that P4 comes from a date a century or so later than P64+67; he claims here and in the book that Kurt Aland, after initially embracing an identification, reversed himself in the matter. The citations offered, however, do not support this claim. Instead, the reality is that Aland never really argued this point and gave his reasons for a position; he just did not take up the identification into his book on the text of the New Testament. He did, it is true, regard the Oxford/Montserrat papyrus and the Paris fragments as different text types, "normal" in the case of P4, "strict" in the case of P64+67. But he elsewhere said that before the late third to early fourth century, the text was "not yet channeled into types"; so the different types mean little, especially with small fragments.[6]

Wachtel points out the weakness of Thiede's position regarding the Paris papyrus, that the style of writing "differs as little from P64 [the Magdalen papyrus] as P67 [the Montserrat papyrus] does," and he notes that Thiede himself dates the Paris fragments around 200. Thiede seems to have recognized quickly that he had left himself exposed by his separation of these pieces, because in the book he places the Paris fragments only a little later than his "earliest" fragments and even attacks others for putting P4 significantly later than the fragments.

Thiede continued, however, to reject the idea that these all came from the same original manuscript. In the book he claims (p. 68) that a study by Philip Comfort decisively disproved any connection (Comfort 1995). This is false. Comfort's article is in fact by no means so definite. He says all three fragments are extremely similar, but he inclines to think P4 and P64+67 are works of the same scribe writing in different codices—but he admits that he is not sure.[7] Thiede in effect plagiarized his arguments in the matter from Comfort: there are slightly thinner strokes in P64+67, there is ecthesis of two characters in P4 instead of one, and the color of the papyrus is darker in P4. But of these the last is irrelevant, easily the product of differing preservation contexts. As Hélène Cuvigny (2009) has observed, even pieces of the same document preserved very close to one another can look very different after many centuries. The other two characteristics are well within the normal range of variation inside a codex.

One other fact was adduced against identity, namely, the fact that the stray fragment bearing the title *kata Matthaion* (according to Matthew) with the Paris papyrus is in a different hand from that of the manuscript's text. But this also is immaterial; it can have been a later addition on the flyleaf, as T. C. Skeat pointed out (1997: 18). It should be kept in mind that the Philo codex, in the binding of which P4 was reused, is dated to the later third century, thus providing a kind of *terminus ante quem* for the Luke codex. And an honest scholar would have noted also that Comfort compared the hand of all three of these fragment groups to *P.Oxy.* 661, a Callimachus text generally dated to the late second or early third century.

The whole matter of the identity of the Paris fragments with the others was dealt with in enormous detail by Skeat the year after the book of Thiede and D'Ancona (Skeat 1997). He provides strong arguments in favor of a single multigospel codex as the source of all these fragments. Moreover, he believed that this was a single-quire codex, which forms a key part of his larger argument that the codex was adopted by Christians as a book form because a single-quire codex could accommodate the four canonical gospels.[8] (See chapter 4 for more on this point.) More recently, Scott Charlesworth has argued that the fiber directions on the surviving fragments of P64+67 and P4 are not consistent with a single-quire codex; although he accepts that they are written by the same scribe, he thinks that they can only belong to separate quires, whether in a single codex or (as he thinks more likely) separate codices (Charlesworth 2007).

I do not want to spend an inordinate amount of time on the book of Thiede and D'Ancona, but it does have some interesting differences from Thiede's article that help to show how the agenda of the article was not the same as the dispassionate style of presentation would suggest. From the start of the book (p. 6), it becomes evident that the objective tone of the article was simply adopted for the occasion; in the book, we find instead a strong personalization of the subject: "[The book] is also the story of Carsten Peter Thiede, whose modern search for answers to academic questions echoes Huleatt's own private pilgrimage." The parallel to the Reverend Charles Huleatt, the purchaser and donor of the Magdalen fragments, can now in retrospect be seen to extend even to ordination into the Anglican clergy and to an early death; Thiede died on December 14, 2004, at the age of fifty-two.

The rest of the agenda, in any case, is up front and occupying center stage in chapter 2, on the dating of the Gospel of Matthew, which is placed before any discussion of the papyrus. This chapter makes it clear that the desire to reopen the question of the date of Matthew has been the driving force all along, and that the previous description of the investigation into the Magdalen papyrus as a routine act of curiosity is disingenuous; it was in fact a deliberate move in a campaign to find a papyrus that could be dated to the first century and thus support the agenda of showing Matthew to be an early composition.

This agenda is, however, less concerned with the specific date of one gospel than with a wide-ranging rejection of modern New Testament scholarship, which is consistently demonized. The most unintentionally hilarious moment comes (p. 24) when the authors say, "On other occasions, outsiders can cause difficulties, which happens from time to time when a New Testament scholar, burdened with scholarly assumption, assumes that he knows more about New Testament papyri than the papyrologist." Indeed! By contrast, classical philology and papyrology play throughout the book the role of good guys; indeed, almost any discipline except New Testament scholarship is good, because it respects evidence. This is claimed even for literary criticism—although it must be admitted that Thiede's idea of literary criticism was Dorothy Sayers (p. 21), something that would leave most literary critics today gaping in surprise.

The central issue of the book, in any case, is the relationship of the gospels to the life of Jesus. "They [ordinary people hearing about Thiede's 'discovery'] were enthralled that the fragments might have been read by men and women who had walked with Jesus through Galilee and wept as the storm gathered above the Cross on Golgotha." Obviously, such persons would have been able to tell the exact truth about Jesus's life and teachings; the possibility that they either might not have all had the same understanding of Jesus or might not have wished to tell the whole truth as they understood it does not seem to have crossed Thiede's mind, but that can be left to the side.

Perhaps the most striking characteristic of the book, simply as a piece of writing, is how many side directions it goes in, whether to fill up space or to deal with vulnerabilities in the argument for re-dating. For example, the history of the codex can hardly be avoided entirely, although it was to a large degree avoided in the *ZPE* article. The early date for the Matthew fragments put forward in the book causes problems for Thiede, because the use of the codex also has to be pushed back to the sixties. At such a date, Thiede says, it would have to represent for Christians a break with Judaism, the roll-using parent of Christianity. This issue does not arise in the *ZPE* article, because there the Matthew fragments are dated to sometime after the destruction of the Temple in 70, the point beyond which Thiede takes it as a given that Christianity and Judaism had parted company. As

Figure 2.4. Qumran fragment 7Q5.
Photo Taila Sagiv, Courtesy of the Israel
Antiquities Authority.

a result, we are presented in the book (p. 51) with an utterly fantastic
tale of a complete Christian-Jewish split during the 60s.[9]

Of course, this is all gratuitous, a problem created in the first place
by the indefensible dating of the Magdalen fragments to the 60s.[10] But
even if one accepted this dating, the problem could be framed very
differently, because it is not at all evident that in this period Christian
writings would have been considered, even by Christians, as similar
in character to the Torah (p. 28). Moreover, I do not think any serious
scholar of early Christianity would defend a view that characterized it
as completely disconnected from Judaism as early as the 60s.

But worse is to come. Once the theory of the adoption of the codex
as a means of distinguishing Christianity from Judaism is advanced,
there is need of evidence that Christians originally used rolls for the
gospels (p. 29). It is thus imperative to demonstrate the existence
of early Christian rolls containing scripture. That leads us back to
Qumran and Thiede's defense of his earlier foray into papyrology in
support of O'Callaghan's identification of 7Q5 as a fragment of Mark,
obviously dating before 70 and a clear indication of Christian use of
the roll for a gospel in the earliest decades after the death of Jesus.[11]

The argument about 7Q5 (figure 2.4), although hardly essential except for the sequence of arguments leading from a date before 70 for
the Magdalen papyrus to an early transition from roll to codex, occupies a lot of space. It rests partly on argument, partly on authority.
Invoking "the Spanish papyrologist José O'Callaghan, the renowned
editor of the Palau-Ribès papyrus collection" is not, it must be said,

of much use; O'Callaghan was a very mediocre papyrologist. Thiede does not disclose that O'Callaghan had in fact tried to identify virtually everything found in cave 7Q as coming from the New Testament, a claim that faced immediate withering attacks and was tacitly withdrawn by O'Callaghan already in 1976. Thiede's other authority is Orsolina Montevecchi, cited (p. 32) from a magazine interview (in *La civiltà cattolica*) as the "last word," who is the only example at this point of the "leading papyrologists" Thiede claims to support identifying 7Q5 as Mark. In another place, Sergio Daris is also invoked. But this entire house of cards was demolished yet again by Hans-Udo Rosenbaum, of the Münster institute so detested by Thiede, in 1987, in a blistering polemic. Apart from various minor distractions, the argument rests on a flagrant misreading of one letter, in this extremely small fragment, adopted in order to get around the fact that nothing else in it obliges us to see it as a fragment of Mark.[12]

The real problem, of course, remains the attempt to date the fragments to the first century in the face of unanimity elsewhere that they should be dated to around the end of the second century.[13] The book admits that the datability to the first century of the Qumran texts (especially the Minor Prophets scroll, 8HevXIIgr) was what attracted Thiede to them as comparative material. If one has that outcome in mind, as Thiede did (p. 117), then this text forms an "ideal" starting point. Herculaneum is also brought into the argument again, with a claim that there was a Christian community at Herculaneum before 79, but no documentation of this claim is offered. Most likely it is a matter of a cross on the wall of a room, which was initially indeed interpreted by some as a Christian symbol but which is in fact almost certainly just the support for a wall cabinet.

Besides Qumran and Herculaneum, Thiede goes on to offer other supposed parallels. One of these is *O.Masada* 784 (figure 2.5); surely derision is the only possible response to this adducing of such a short and poorly written text to compare with a well-written manuscript. But, of course, we know when Masada fell. Another is *P.Oxy.* II 246, conveniently dated to 66. Although papyrologists are repeatedly praised in the book for their lack of an agenda, this praise applies only to papyrologists in the abstract. In the form of real individuals, papyrologists have never accepted Thiede's redating. Graham Stanton

Figure 2.5. *O.Masada* 784. Photo Mariana Salzberger, Courtesy of the Israel Antiquities Authority.

(1995: 196 n. 15) reports on the expert advice he received on this point from Peter Parsons, who convened a group of papyrologists to discuss it. All of them dated the codex to the third century, except for one who hesitatingly preferred the fourth. That late a date seems difficult to me because of the generally accepted date for the Philo codex in the Bibliothèque nationale in the cover of which the Luke fragments were reused.

I am afraid this becomes tedious, to risk an English pun. But I do not want to leave this subject without mentioning an interesting sidelight on the impact of Thiede's desire to assign earlier dates to biblical fragments. In 2000, Amphilochios Papathomas published a fragment of the letter to the Hebrews from the Vienna papyrus collection (figure 2.6). He remarked (p. 20), "The fragment can be safely dated by applying palaeographical criteria. In fact, even though several characteristics of the elegant script point to an early dating, the drawing of specific letters such as ε and μ allows us to date the papyrus to the sixth or seventh century." He offered several specific parallels for the dating that he proposed.

The following year, a professor of Old Testament and theology, Karl Jaroš, offering his thanks for advice to Carsten Thiede, proposed instead to date the papyrus to the late second or early third century

Figure 2.6. P.Vindob. G 42417: Letter to the Hebrews. Photo courtesy Papyrussammlung, Österreichische Nationalbibliothek.

(Jaroš 2001). Unlike Papathomas, he judges the script to be without elegance and indeed not even the product of a professional scribe, being instead the work of a slow writer. He adduces palaeographical parallels for his date, although these parallels in fact come from professionally produced works. He also suggests that the scribe's use of abbreviation of divine names is more at home in an earlier period than a later, although to this again one might reply that if the scribe is as amateurish as Jaroš thinks, such arguments are not very compelling. Indeed, he sees the inconsistent usage here as a reflection of dogmatic controversies in Alexandria in the early third century. Overinterpretation, I think one might say.

We may now turn to something altogether more substantive and positive, where we shall be dealing in the main with good, even excellent, scholarship and real, rather than phony, problems. But the issues raised by this material are nonetheless full of troubling and difficult aspects concerning the earliest stratum of Christian books. They will also introduce us more concretely to the great question of the early history of the codex in Christian usage, which will occupy us in the final chapter.

Volume 69 of the *Oxyrhynchus Papyri* presents three previously unpublished papyri, each containing a part of the *Shepherd* of Hermas, edited with customary precision by Nikolaos Gonis. According to his reckoning, these three papyri join twenty others of that work previously known. This count omits Codex Sinaiticus (LDAB 3478), made of parchment, in which Hermas was appended to the Old and New Testaments; it also does not include the latest manuscript of Hermas listed in the Leuven Database of Ancient Books (8595), a codex of the eighth century now part of the Düsseldorf University Library but originally from the north of England. Two of the new texts are for our purposes of particular interest, because they are rolls.

Table 2.1 shows the distribution of the dates attributed to these twenty-three papyri by the Leuven Database. It is hardly necessary to emphasize that this chronological distribution is entirely different from that of Christian books in general, and indeed from the model presented in chapter 1 for the number of Christian books that one might expect from a growing population of Christians between the second and fourth centuries. Half of the witnesses to Hermas can be dated before the turn of the third to fourth centuries. Even viewed in the light of the general tendency that we have observed for the dates of Christian papyri to be pushed earlier, this chronological distribution is peculiar to Hermas and is unlikely to be completely mistaken.

Hermas occupies a unique place in the literature of the first Christian centuries. Although Hermas ultimately was not included in the

TABLE 2.1
Distribution of Dates Attributed to 23 Hermas Papyri by the Leuven Database

Date attributed in the LDAB	Number of texts
II/III	3
III	6
III/IV	2
IV	4
IV/V	3
V	2
V/VI	1
VI	2

FIGURE 2.7. *P.Iand.* I 4. Photo courtesy Universitätsbibliothek, Giessen.

Christian scriptural canon, at least his inclusion in the Codex Sinaiticus shows that he was viewed in some circles as worthy of inclusion with the scriptures. The text of the *Shepherd,* however, seems to have been considerably less fixed than that of the gospels or of the Pauline letters. And it is striking that four of the twenty-three surviving witnesses are rolls. Two of these texts are written on the versos of rolls of which the rectos had already been used for other texts. This is a phenomenon of recycling well known for classical literature and indeed known even for the canonical scriptures. But two of the witnesses of Hermas are written on new rolls, the other side of which is blank. For the canonical scriptures, there is no parallel for this practice. We shall return to this aspect of Hermas later on in discussing the development of the codex.

For the moment we shall concentrate on a problem raised by Antonio Carlini (1992), namely, the date of *P.Iand.* I 4 (figure 2.7), a fragment originally identified as coming from an unknown medical text but later attributed to Hermas independently by Michael Gronewald and Jean Lenaerts. It figures in the Leuven Database among the texts dated to the end of the second or the beginning of the third century, thus belonging to the first group in table 2.1. The date given in the first edition of the text was the fourth century. Lenaerts later proposed more precisely the beginning of the fourth century. Carlini, invoking an unpublished communication presented by Peter Parsons to the International Congress of Classical Studies in Dublin (1984), raised the further question whether a date that late was possible or if, instead, the date of the papyrus ought to be placed much earlier, perhaps even in the first half of the second century. He cited parallels for the second half of the first century, indeed, but preferred a somewhat later date.

A rather considerable correspondence ensued, which Carlini summarizes in his article (1992: 23–24). The opinions of various scholars diverge considerably. Guglielmo Cavallo thinks it difficult to accept any date later than the middle of the second century, but Gronewald is unwilling to go earlier than the end of that century. Several of the scholars who participated in the discussion, Parsons himself first of all, ask if deliberate archaism could have produced the impression of a hand of the second century; Parsons also mentions the possibility of "incompetence," offering *P.Oxy.* L 3529 (figure 2.8) as an example.

Carlini then sets out the troubling consequences of such an early date, in the following words (I translate his Italian original): "An insurmountable difficulty to a date in the first half of the second century for a papyrus of the Shepherd arises at once from the traditional information concerning the composition of Hermas's work: according to the detailed notice contained in the Muratorian Canon, the date of composition should fall between 142 and 155, when Pius, the brother of Hermas, occupied the [episcopal] seat of the Church of Rome."[14]

Because the Muratorian Canon is to be dated, in all probability, toward the end of the second century, its testimony cannot easily be abandoned or rejected for lack of authority.[15] If one accepts its information, however, and if the date of this fragment of Hermas is to be placed around the middle of the century, it follows that, as Carlini puts it, "the time available for the diffusion of the work to Egypt is very short with respect to the date of publication."

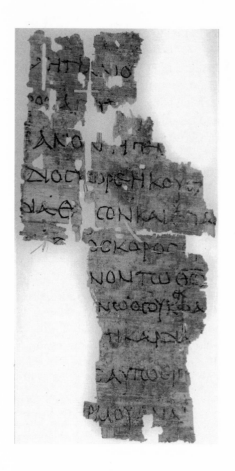

FIGURE 2.8. *P.Oxy.* L 3529. Photo courtesy of the Egypt Exploration Society.

At this point the reasons for which I decided to juxtapose the case of the fragments of Matthew and the saga of Carsten Thiede with that of Hermas may be evident. In both cases, the dates attributed by the editors of these texts are rejected in favor of a much earlier date, with very important consequences for the dates of composition and dissemination of a central work in Christian literature. There is disagreement among experts about the correct date. It is not difficult to imagine a slippery slope into relativism and despair before us. As Carlini himself put it, "Should we then close the problem and declare that a dating on a palaeographic basis that is in conflict with the testimony of a detailed tradition may not be proposed?" (Carlini 1992: 25).

No one will be surprised to find that Carlini's question is rhetorical, and that he resolves his dilemma by following a different path. He observes that the *Shepherd* was, from its beginning, anything but a unified work. It is, rather, a combination of two originally autonomous collections. One of these is made up of the four books of the *Visions*, and the other of the *Precepts* and *Similitudes*, with the addition, by way of preface, of what is generally numbered as the fifth book of the *Visions*. Carlini provides a list of the papyrus codices that one can show, or at least argue with some probability, to have contained only one of these two original works. This list includes *P.Mich.* 129 and *P.Oxy.* L 3527 and 3528, all of which included only the *Precepts* and the *Similitudes*. All three manuscripts, to which may be added the Giessen papyrus (*P.Iand.* 4), which comes also from this section of the *Shepherd*, may be classed among the oldest manuscripts of Hermas. There are other, later witnesses, both direct and indirect, for the continued circulation of a text without *Visions* I–IV. Carlini remarks, moreover, that the name of Hermas is found in the text only of *Visions* I–IV; moreover, the vocative *adelphoi* (brothers) occurs only in the same books, a word that, in his view, "shows the close relationship with the Roman community."

In the same spirit and with the same approach toward the tradition of Hermas, and following as well some observations that go back at least as far as the edition of *P.Mich.* 130 by Campbell Bonner, Carlini also argues that there was a high level of variability or of polymorphism in the first circulated texts of Hermas. As he says, the text "for its reconstruction entirely escapes . . . the network of Lachmanian and Maasian rules."[16]

It is this Michigan papyrus (figure 2.9), written on the back of a roll containing on its recto a register of landed property, that, according to Carlini, is to be dated to the end of the second century rather than the third century, and which provoked his study of polymorphism. According to Carlini, then, neither the fundamental structure of the book nor the details of its text were stably unified; the *Shepherd* becomes thus more and more a protean text, in which what we conceive of as the normal rules are not in effect. Carlini attributes these characteristics to the "unauthorized" or "private" dissemination of the text.

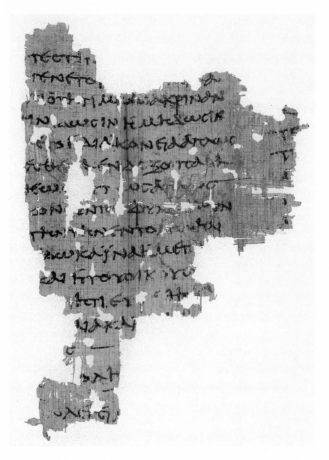

Figure 2.9. *P.Mich.* 130. Photo courtesy University of Michigan Library.

It remains uncertain, in my view, what these terms mean in such a context. Even *P.Mich.* 130, despite its irregularities when one compares it with the text as it is known from other, more complete but also later texts, seems to be the work of a well-educated scribe, accustomed to copying Christian texts. It is possible that this polymorphism was less widespread than Carlini thinks, but the best-preserved text among the newly published Oxyrhynchus papyri, *P.Oxy.* LXIX 4706, contains many textual variants, without conforming to any of the later manuscripts.

If the two parts of the *Shepherd* circulated separately, it becomes possible to interpret the notice of the Muratorian Canon about the publication of the work under Pius as a reference to the publication of an edition of the two parts in a single book, a hypothesis that would permit the circulation of the individual components in separate editions before 155. A fragment dating from the middle of the century could thus perfectly well be, as far as we can tell, a piece of such an earlier partial edition. This hypothesis offers us a way out from otherwise unavoidable difficulties, arising from the contradiction between the testimony about the date of publication and the wish to date the fragment to an early date. To be sure, it will be obvious that this hypothesis requires us in a sense to interpret the Muratorian Canon tendentiously, in order to find there the indication wanted—that is, in order to save the palaeographic date attributed to the papyrus fragment. Methodologically, one may find this at best somewhat awkward.

Into this state of the discussion enters *P.Oxy.* LXIX 4706, "twenty-seven fragments of a roll, blank on the back," as its editor, Gonis, says. Of these fragments, only seventeen have been placed so far. Gonis describes the hand as "informal with cursive tendencies, of the kind that C. H. Roberts described as 'reformed documentary' . . . I would assign it to the first part of the third century, though I would not exclude a date in the very end of the second." The identified fragments contain portions of books III and IV of the *Visions* and almost all the books of the *Precepts* (*Mandata*), from which only books I and III are lacking. Gonis remarks, "The original roll must have contained the *Visiones* as well as the *Mandata* (it is less likely that we have fragments of two different rolls). Compare the *Codex Sinaiticus*, which contained all three parts of the *Pastor*. This is of some interest, since it has repeatedly been argued that *Mandata* and *Similitudines* circulated independently of *Visiones* I–IV (*Vis.* V serving as an introduction to *Mand.* and *Sim.*); contrast, however, Aland and Rosenbaum, *Repertorium* pp. lxxxvii–xciv, especially the codicological part of their argument."

Gonis does not take this argument further, and we cannot enter here into the details of such a complicated controversy. But the obvious reply to Gonis's remarks from the separatist point of view is that an instance of a unified edition produced at the end of the second century or the start of the third does not pose any difficulty, because the unified edition will have existed in any case since the 150s and will thus have circulated for four or five decades before the date of the Oxyrhynchus roll. There is obviously no reason, moreover, why separate editions of the two halves of the *Shepherd* cannot have continued to circulate after the omnibus edition became available, just as the establishment of the canon of the New Testament did not produce the disappearance of codices with a single book in favor of complete Bibles. We know that the contrary is true: separate copies of individual books or of groups of books of the Bible continued to be made and read alongside the great codices that contained the entire Old and New Testaments, or only the New Testament. Probably the cost of books played a role (for this argument, see chapter 3). Tastes, needs, and individual convenience were also important. But it is at least clear that from the time of the bishop Demetrios the totality of the *Shepherd* could have been acquired in a single volume. Whatever the worth of the later witnesses to the circulation of individual parts, we have no reason to doubt the existence of complete editions.

In insisting on the structural similarities of the two controversies that I have presented in this chapter, I have up to a certain point been teasing. These similarities exist, and they remind us again how vulnerable the datings of ancient literary manuscripts can be to radical attack. Even among competent scholars without any tendentious program, it can be difficult to arrive at a consensus, even an approximate consensus. Opinions can diverge by a century or even more. At the same time, it is only fair to say that even if the structures of the two controversies are not entirely different, the scientific methodologies involved have hardly a single point in common. Thiede's argument in his article is a kind of burlesque of a normal scholarly presentation, just as his book is a parody of a work of academic popularization. In the case of Hermas and *P.Iand.* 4, we find ourselves listening in on a discussion among colleagues, a conversation that produces a substantial degree of convergence on the character of the writing. Consensus is less evident on the date to be assigned, but the foundations of the disagreement are located for the most part in the extent to which the scholars are willing to invoke one of the possible exit routes proposed by Peter Parsons—that is, archaism or incompetence. It is noteworthy that many of those who contributed to this debate qualified their opinions, referring to the small sample available and to their dependence on photographs instead of being able to see the original manuscripts before offering an opinion.

I would not wish to suggest that majority vote is the best means of discovering the best answer to questions of scholarly judgment. The use of such votes in the notorious Jesus Seminar organized by the late Robert Funk—a bête noire for Thiede if there ever was one, I suppose—has provoked much derision in the popular press, and no doubt also among scholars in New Testament studies with a different methodological allegiance. All the same, respect for the opinions of the scientific community is a good thing, and it is sensible to pay attention to the dominant point of view particularly in cases when differing views rest on inconclusive proofs. The love of seeing himself as a *vox clamantis in eremo* so visible in Thiede, the self-identification as the only one who dares to speak the truth, is self-interested; it is better to be characterized as a prophet by others than to proclaim oneself a prophet. But it is perhaps still not entirely a bad thing for papyrologists to remember that much can depend on palaeographic datings, and that editors should take care that such datings rest on as strong a foundation as possible, a group of parallels as precise as available, and as wide a consensus as possible.

CHAPTER III
The Economics of Book Production

In the first chapter, while considering the numbers of Christian manuscripts likely to have existed in Egypt in the second and third centuries, and the chances that they would have survived to come into our hands and would have been edited, I remarked briefly on some of the ways in which Christian books differed from classical literature in their audience and uses. These differences have consequences for the numbers of books likely to have been created. The most important difference was of course that Christian books had no role in the traditional Greek educational system of these centuries. Thus no copies would have been made for ownership by teachers, for use in schools, or for later reading by educated individuals who wanted to read the works with which they were familiar from their education.

One external constraint on the production and circulation of books was certainly cost.[1] Whether books were Christian or not, they cost money to produce, and someone had to find that money. The cost of books and the nature of the book trade in antiquity are also well-trodden scholarly ground, but I have never been satisfied that the discussions of this subject have been based on sufficient grasp of the workings of ancient prices and incomes, and I think it is worth the trouble to look at the subject again. Because the potential cost savings of monastic production have become a standard topic in such discussions, we need to understand as well as possible what those savings might have been. The cost relationship between parchment and papyrus is also worth further consideration; this, of course, is also significant for the discussion of the early history of the codex to which we shall turn in chapter 4.

Actual book prices are only rarely preserved, and when they are mentioned it is sometimes in contexts where we should be cautious about taking them literally. The most famous book for which a value is mentioned is probably the complete parchment Bible owned by Abba Gelasios and mentioned in the *Apophthegmata Patrum* (*PG* 65, 145 [Alph.]), where it is said to have been valued at 18 gold solidi, or 72 Roman grams of gold, the solidus having been 4 grams from the time of Constantine onward. John Moschus (*Pratum spirituale* 134, *PG* 87/3.2997) refers to a New Testament valued at 3 solidi. That would value this New Testament at one-sixth (16⅔ percent) of the total value of Gelasios's Bible. The New Testament is in fact a bit over 19 percent of the total length of the Bible; 3 solidi for the New Testament would imply a value of 15.6 solidi for the whole Bible, only a little less than the value reported for Gelasios's Bible. These figures need not be taken as factual, of course, coming as they do from spiritually improving monastic literature where exaggeration might have been useful for making a point, but their internal consistency is impressive. There is also a reference in the *Acta Conciliorum Oecumenicorum* indicating that a Latin copy of the Acts of the Fifth Council had been bought from an aristocrat for 6 solidi (*ACO* II.2.2, p. 650).

At the other end of the cost spectrum are references in Theban West Bank ostraka of the seventh century to books costing one tremissis (*trimesion* in Greek and Coptic), or a third of a solidus. I am indebted to Anne Boud'hors for information about these prices.[2] She notes that this price typically represents an unbound book; binding would normally double the cost. She regards this as a substantial sum, in comparison, for example, with normal tax burdens for individuals. It is, of course, only a tiny fraction of the prices that I have just been quoting. A proportional calculation, however, suggests that it is not necessarily out of line with them. Gelasios's splendid parchment Bible cost 18 solidi. We may reckon that for this price he acquired a bound volume containing approximately 765,379 words—I assume that his Bible containing the Old and New Testaments included the Apocryphal books. The proportionate contents purchasable with one tremissis, or ¹/₅₄ of the value of Gelasios's Bible, would be 14,174 words. That assumes, however, the highest-quality book production, including binding. Even so, one could have acquired the Gospel of Mark (12,076 words), or all the non-Pauline letters, or Job, or any number of other assemblages of shorter books. On the assumption that these books mentioned in the Coptic ostraka are relatively short ones, not complete Bibles, the price fits with our information from literary sources.

At the same time, however, this calculation raises the question of the relative cost of papyrus and parchment. Boud'hors cites the often-discussed limestone ostrakon *SBKopt.* I 12, with its inventory of the books of an otherwise unknown *topos*, probably a monastery. It consisted of about forty-five books on papyrus and thirteen on parchment, or more than three-quarters on papyrus. These books, not surprisingly, mostly consisted of individual books of the Bible or combinations of them: Judges, for example, at 16,883 words, is combined with Ruth, at only 2,200, to form a book of about 19,000 words on papyrus. There is one four-gospel parchment manuscript, no doubt the most valuable book in the library. At all events, we need to understand what part in the production of books was played by the raw materials used, as compared to the cost of labor.

We possess one price for parchment from the Edict on Maximum Prices (7.38) issued by Diocletian in 301, where a *quaternio* measuring a foot square (that is, about 30 cm on a side) is listed at 40 denarii maximum: *membranario in [qua]t[erni]one pedali pergamen[i vel] croca[ti]*, a text partly restored and corrected but based on the survival of the critical words in the Greek version, most notably τετράδα μ[ονόπουν].[3] In the same Edict (1.1a) wheat is priced at 100 denarii per modius, which gives us a useful standard for comparing other prices and incomes—more useful than the golden coin, the aureus, in fact, because it is highly unlikely that the price for that in the Edict reflects actual market value at the time. A modius was thus worth 2.5 *quaterniones*. For Egyptian measurement, converting modii to artabas[4] at a rate of 10 modii per 3 artabas allows us to see that an artaba was worth $8\frac{1}{3}$ *quaterniones*. The Constantinian gold solidus in the fourth century normally would buy 8 artabas of wheat, so a solidus would have bought $66\frac{2}{3}$ *quaterniones*, or $266\frac{2}{3}$ sheets. As always in such calculations, room must be allowed for approximation and variation.

A second price is given in *P.Oxy.* XVII 2156, a letter assigned by the editors to the late fourth or early fifth century, in which the writer speaks of the purchase of 25 *tetradia*—the Greek term for *quaterniones*—of unspecified dimensions at a rate of 14 talents. If that number is taken at face value as the price per *quaternio*, we could proceed to calculate that the solidus must be valued at 66²/₃ *quaterniones* per solidus times 14 talents per *quaternio*, yielding a result of 933¹/₃ talents per solidus and thus the pound of gold at 67,203 talents (933¹/₃ × 72). That is an impossible figure for any time after 351 and not easy to locate in the monetary history of the period before 351, either (Bagnall 1985: 37–48). In the period to which the papyrus is assigned, in fact, the price of gold in talents was more than ten times this amount. It is true that there is a possible two-letter lacuna in the text after the numeral 14, but that would at best be the place for a fraction and thus of no material help to us. (The editor remarks that in fact nothing may have been written there.) Unfortunately, the papyrus is lost, and no photograph is available. It is thus impossible to verify either the assigned date or the readings. It would, perhaps, be possible to argue that the price given is not per *tetradion* but for the entire 25 of them making up the *diphthera*; the wording is not entirely clear: τὴν διφθέραν [τ]ῶν μεμβρανῶν ἐν τετραδίοις εἰκ[οσ]ιπέντε τιμῆς ἀργυρίου (ταλάντων) ιδ [. . .]. In that case, 14 talents should equal the fraction of a solidus that these *quaterniones* were worth, or three-eighths on the assumption that a solidus bought 66²/₃. That would put the solidus at 37¹/₃ talents, or the pound of gold at 2,688 talents. That price level would belong to the period 325–330. That would be quite a bit earlier than the "late fourth or fifth century" date assigned by the editor, but I do not think we can dismiss the possibility out of hand.

Sigrid Mratschek has applied the price for parchment given in the Edict of Maximum Prices that we have been using to a report of Cassiodorus that his translation of the entire Bible (the Septuagint and New Testament) could be accommodated in a codex composed of 95 *quaterniones*. She supposes that these are the same type mentioned in the Edict, and she thus calculates a total cost in Diocletianic terms of 3,800 denarii, which she equates to 3¹/₆ Diocletianic aurei. Even though the outcome of this calculation is not far from what I believe to be correct, the calculation itself cannot be accepted as yielding a usable result, in part because it does not take account of the serious problems posed by the underpricing of the aureus in the Edict.

Equally important is the question of the amount of parchment. I do not know how many words Cassiodorus's translation came to, but the Greek original is, as I noted earlier, about 765,000 words.[5] The 95 *quaterniones* would be 380 sheets, which when folded would come to 1,520 pages. The resultant book must have had about 500 words per page in order to accommodate the entire Bible.

Such a figure is credible for what Cassiodorus describes as *codice grandiore, littera clariore conscripto* (1.14.2). But the *quaterniones* mentioned by the Edict would have made a codex about 15 cm wide and 30 cm high, which in *litterae clariores* could not have held more than 40 lines per page at 6 words per line, and might well have held less, like *P.Chester Beatty* VII, which at 26 cm high had only 25–26 lines of between 5 and 6 words each. Such a book would not quite accommodate half of Cassiodorus's text. Obviously what Cassiodorus has in mind must have been something more like Codex Vaticanus or Codex Sinaiticus. We must therefore take *grandior* seriously. Guglielmo Cavallo has estimated that Codex Sinaiticus originally consisted of about 730 folios or a bit more, each about 72 by 38 centimeters, thus a book of almost exactly the size I am supposing for Cassiodorus. With about 48 lines to a page and four columns of about 13 characters each, it has some 2,500 characters per page. (Codex Vaticanus has a smaller page size, although that is in part the result of trimming.)

In the 30 cm format sheets, by contrast, with a single column, the Greek Bible would have occupied more like 3,400 pages, or 850 sheets, or 213 *quaterniones*. That calculation assumes 225 words per page. That would mean a cost in terms of the Edict of Maximum Prices of 213 *quaterniones* × 40 denarii each, or 8,520 denarii, the value of 85 modii of grain. In terms of the Constantinian solidus, the result would be 3.2 solidi (213 divided by 66⅔) for the total amount of 766,800 square cm of parchment, or 1,533,600 square cm of writable surface, counting both sides. If we compare this figure of 3.2 solidi for a complete Bible with the values for books canvassed above, it will be evident that the cost of the parchment would have come to about 18 percent of the cost of the book. We do not have parchment prices for the larger sheets used in the great codices, however; probably the cost for larger sheets, which required larger skins, was higher for each unit of area. A parchment cost of about 20 percent of the cost of the book thus seems like a minimum figure for such grand codices.

By way of comparison, it may be estimated that the standard papyrus roll offered 30,000 square cm on both sides: 30 cm high, or about the same as the foot used to measure the sheets of parchment, and composed of 20 sheets of about 25 cm width each. (Rolls of other lengths certainly existed, but Skeat [1982] has argued persuasively that undifferentiated references to papyrus rolls should refer to the 20-sheet standard.) Because these sheets are overlapped in order to glue them together to make a roll, however, Skeat has calculated an average net of about 17 cm writable width per sheet, or 340 cm per roll. Each roll would therefore yield about 11 sheets of 30 by 30 cm like the parchment ones mentioned above, or the equivalent of 2¾ *quaterniones*. It would therefore require about 78 papyrus rolls to provide the space necessary for the entire Bible in the same format.

For papyrus prices from the fourth century, we have a price of 3⅓ talents per roll in *SB* XIV 11583, which can be dated circa 338–341. At that time, wheat cost 24 talents per artaba, so one could buy 7.2 rolls for the price of an artaba. That is, just under 11 artabas would pay for the papyrus needed for a Bible. In solidi, about one and a third solidi would suffice for the papyrus. Parchment on this reckoning was not quite two and a half times as expensive as papyrus. Another price for papyrus is found in *P.Panop.* 19 x, from 342, or just slightly later than the other papyrus. Here it is double the other amount, or 6⅔ talents per roll. There had certainly been an upward tick in general price levels in the brief interval between the two documents, but we have little evidence from these years to help contextualize the number. Another problem is that the word for papyrus is modified in the Panopolite receipt by an apparently abbreviated Greek word, αδη, which the editors left unresolved and described as "unintelligible to us." It is not one of the terms used to indicate a longer than normal roll listed by Skeat (1982), and the editors reject their only guess, ἄδη(κτοι), "worm-eaten," because it is unknown in documentary Greek.[6]

Copying, by contrast, would have cost the same on the two media. If we make the perhaps rash assumption that the lines of copying envisaged by the Edict on Maximum Prices were of the width to occupy the sheets of parchment mentioned in the same edict, we hear that 100 lines at the grade just below the best writing would have cost 20 denarii. (This may not seem such a rash assumption, however; the figures for the cost of scribal copying in the Edict follow the price of parchment immediately in the text.) As we are talking about the Bible, a text that should have occupied 136,677 such lines, the cost would come to 27,335 denarii. That is 273 modii of wheat, or 82 artabas, or about 10 solidi. At the higher price of 25 denarii per 100 lines, the cost would be 34,169 denarii, or 342 modii of wheat, 102 artabas, or a bit under 13 solidi. Since the biblical codex worth 18 solidi belonging to Abba Gelasios was undoubtedly bound, and the binding will have added a significant amount, we may like to imagine that Gelasios had second-quality rather than first-quality copying in his book. But the margin for error in all these numbers is enough to leave that uncertain.

When we think about more ordinary books, we should note that the Edict gives a price of 10 denarii per 100 lines of *scriptura libelli vel tabularum*. This price can only with difficulty be referred to any standard width of text; certainly there is no standardization in petitions preserved on papyrus, which can have narrow formats or wide ones. This may also remind us that we do not know what line width the calligraphers were producing. It must also be observed, moreover, that we do not actually know to what standard of writing the grades in the Edict refer. Some petitions, after all, are elegantly written; others are hastily scribbled.

Another approach is offered by Skeat using a figure for documentary writing preserved in an account from the first half of the third century, where the cost for 10,000 lines, *stichoi*, is given as 28 drachmas, and the cost for one particular actual task was 47 drachmas; the amount of writing involved is only partly preserved but seems inescapably restored as 16,600 *stichoi*. If the date assigned to the account is correct, we should use an average wheat price of 16 drachmas per artaba to provide perspective on the cost of copying.[7] That would mean that 10,000 lines cost 1¾ artabas, or 5⅚ modii, which would have cost 583 denarii at the time of the Edict of Maximum Prices, whereas the price for the *tabellio*, the lowest quality specified in the Edict, would have been 1,000 denarii. In other words, the cost of formal legal documents and petitions at the rates in the Edict is nearly double that of the writing referred to in the London account, leaving aside once again questions of the length of the line, which cannot be resolved. It is entirely plausible to suppose that the ordinary account-writing at stake in the lower price represents a level of labor that the imperial government did not bother to regulate in the Edict.

Taking all this information together, table 3.1 summarizes the cost estimates in solidi for a complete Bible, assuming the various possible choices of material and quality of writing but not including binding, which, as we have seen, would add a tremissis for a small book and no doubt much more for a large one—perhaps a solidus for a full Bible.

The relative price advantage of papyrus obviously depended on the cost of the labor, that is, on the degree of quality of scribal work one was prepared to pay for. At one end of the spectrum, for a first-quality book production, the difference between papyrus and parchment was only 12.5 percent. Probably no one who spent that much on copyists would need to save that small amount. If one was prepared to invest that much in copyists, it would make sense to choose the more luxurious material also. At the other end of the spectrum, using parchment would add 50 percent to the cost of a book copied by an ordinary documentary scribe. That would be a significant cost difference. Of course these figures are for a full Bible, which would be

TABLE 3.1
Cost Estimates (in Solidi) for One Bible

	Calligraphic	Second quality	Tabellio	Documentary
Cost of labor	12.8	10.2	5.1	3.0
Cost of parchment	3.2	3.2	3.2	3.2
Cost of papyrus	1.3	1.3	1.3	1.3
Total cost, on parchment	16.0	13.4	8.3	6.2
Total cost, on papyrus	14.0	11.5	6.4	4.3

a massive undertaking on any assumptions; even with documentary writing quality and papyrus, the amount of money at stake in making such a book was considerable. At all events, the figures are sufficiently close to those reported in the literary sources for the cost of books that we may have some level of comfort in concluding that they are close to what people would actually have experienced. They can be scaled down to smaller books with little difficulty; economies of scale would have affected mainly the binding.

To these considerations we must add a reminder that papyrus was sometimes recycled. Even papyrus was therefore not cheap enough that its cost was unimportant. Nor should we assume that only the poor or pupils in school recycled papyrus. Very much the contrary is true. The reuse of obsolete documentary rolls for classical literature written on their backs is a well-known phenomenon. It has been debated whether such recycling reflects a commercial trade in used papyrus or instead the private use of papyrus to which an individual had access. That such a commercial trade existed is asserted by Ewa Wipszycka in a recent article (2000: 188–89), in which she says, "we know quite well that waste paper trade existed in antiquity," but without offering any evidence or bibliography. Whatever may be the origin of the documents used inside the covers of the Nag Hammadi codices for stiffening, which Wipszycka attributes to such a commercial trade, I believe that the second of these explanations—private, or internal, recycling—is the correct one in most cases. It is certainly difficult otherwise to explain cases in which a roll originally written in one place is found in a distant location with a literary work on the other side. Presumably if one went to a shop in Oxyrhynchus to buy used papyrus, one would get discarded Oxyrhynchite documents. One case from my own experience is the census register from Lykopolis reused for the text of Pindar's Paeans, which was found by Grenfell and Hunt at Oxyrhynchus. It seems very likely that this roll was simply taken by an Oxyrhynchite serving in an official capacity in Lykopolis sometime in the early second century, once it no longer seemed to him necessary in the archives.[8]

I have already mentioned in earlier chapters several cases in which Christian texts, even the scriptures, were written on the backs of previously used rolls; these are our only instances of the scriptures in roll form. The practice did not disappear with the dominance of the codex, but obviously the normal practice of writing on both sides of the page in a codex eliminated the simple opportunities for reuse that the roll had presented. A parchment codex, of course, would stand up to having the text washed out and replaced. But with papyrus this is not a normal event. The one good way to recycle a codex that had fallen apart, in fact, was to use it as stuffing inside the binding of a new codex. This is what happened with the fragments of the Gospel of Luke in the Bibliothèque nationale de France, which I have discussed briefly in chapter 2; they were put into the binding of a codex containing the works of Philo.

At the end of the third and the beginning of the fourth century, of course, there were still many rolls, both documentary and literary, in archives and libraries. When the codex became at this time much more widely used, someone had the clever idea of gluing the written sides of two rolls together, creating a double-thickness roll with two blank sides, both with vertical fibers. This arrangement must have produced the raw material for codices of very undistinguished quality, rather thicker than was normal. We owe to Jean Gascou the identification of this practice as one closely linked to a standard page format used in Panopolis, from which all the known examples come (Gascou 1989; Bagnall 2002a). The raw materials were registers related to contracts and taxation, as well as official correspondence, which came from public archives in Panopolis. Some of the codices made from this material were used for private documentary purposes, but most of the ones we know have literary texts, both Christian and classical. They give us clear evidence that in the circles that produced these books, which have not yet been identified with any degree of confidence, the cost of papyrus was a sufficient consideration to warrant the labor of gluing the old rolls together rather than simply buying new ones and to make it acceptable to put up with less than optimum quality in the raw material.

As a final piece in this part of the discussion, I must return to the question whether monastic labor lowered the cost of book production and gave monasteries an advantage in becoming dominant centers of book production. No doubt when the additional evidence from ostraka from the Theban region is published we will have a somewhat better idea about this question. But it seems to me that we must distinguish between monks copying manuscripts so that their own monasteries could have copies for their libraries and monks copying manuscripts on commission for external individuals or institutions (Kotsifou 2007; Koenen 1974). It is entirely possible that the first case meant that scribal labor was in a sense free for monasteries. But all labor nonetheless represented a kind of opportunity cost for the monastery, a missed chance to earn revenue to support the monks and the monastery.[9] With respect to external buyers, on the other hand, one can only say that there is no evidence that monasteries actually charged less than anyone else, and if the books costing a tremissis were, as I suppose, of the type found both in most surviving manuscripts and in the inventories, individual books of the Bible and texts of similar length, then the price does not seem out of line with other prices we have.

We must turn now to consider what these figures mean in terms of wealth and incomes. Just how expensive were books? Many customers for Christian books were, in modern terms, institutional: churches and monasteries. No doubt we have a disproportionate amount of information about their libraries. The books belonging to churches are mentioned in accounts of persecutions of the church under Diocletian, and monasteries have been a disproportionately important source of surviving manuscript fragments and of information about the making and acquiring of books, thanks in large part to the fact that so many of them were located in the desert fringes of the Nile valley and thus were dryer than most other locations. We have no good basis for judging the financial resources of most monasteries, above all for deciding how much money they had left over after the highest priorities: feeding the monks, maintaining their physical facilities, and doing whatever deeds of charity for the community they thought important. No doubt monastic institutional wealth varied almost as much as personal wealth. So, surely, did the wealth of parish churches.

About the resources of the churches and monasteries in the fourth century we know almost nothing. Here and there we find signs that these institutions were beginning to acquire land,[10] but nothing allows us to quantify these possessions. By the sixth century, we can at least know what the imperial government thought the revenues of churches were, because in *Novel* 143, of 546, Justinian described seven categories of churches, ranked by annual revenue. The first is made up of the five patriarchal churches. Below these were six bands:

2. Metropolitan seats: more than 2,160 solidi (30 lbs.)
3. 720–2,160 solidi (10–30 lbs.)
4. 360–720 solidi (5–10 lbs.)
5. 216–360 solidi (3–5 lbs.)
6. 144–216 solidi (2–3 lbs.)
7. Less than 144 solidi (2 lbs.)

Of course, we have only limited information about the operating budgets of these churches. We know that salaries of the clergy and charity for the poor were among the main purposes for which the bishops had to spend the income of their churches. Village churches presumably for the most part had revenue levels well below the figures given in the table, which refer to episcopal seats, usually in cities. It seems likely that the first three classes had adequate resources to acquire whatever books they needed, but below that level it is not difficult to imagine that other expenses consumed most of what was available. For monasteries, we have as far as I know nothing like the information that this *Novel* of Justinian offers for the episcopal churches. At the same time, the inventories like the one from the West Bank at Thebes to which I referred earlier show that some monasteries, at least, did acquire a good library of biblical texts and some other theological literature in addition.

Among individuals, I suggested earlier what must seem obvious, namely, that the clergy were the most likely possessors of Christian books. We have a recent survey of the evidence for the incomes of the clergy in Sabine Hübner's book on the clergy in the society of late antique Asia Minor—which in fact covers evidence from a wider range than its title might suggest (Hübner 2005: 213–25). We have no indication if the rule favored by the papacy was used in the East, whereby the bishop and the lower clergy each received a quarter of the total revenues, the rest going to church maintenance and to charity. As A.H.M. Jones pointed out, the rule was not uniformly used in the West, either.[11] If it is used as a guide, it can be seen that many of the churches in the lower rungs of the scale will not have had a lot to divide up. The richer churches would have had much more ample resources, of course, but Hübner remarks that any increase in the number of clergy in a church would imply a decline in the income of the existing officeholders. And these churches did have substantial staffs. Apamea in Syria had seventy-seven members of the clergy in 518. This was of course a grand urban center, and it is not unexpected to find a large staff there.[12] Overall, Hübner suggests on the basis of a variety of calculations that produce converging results that the higher clergy, the priests and deacons, probably on average tended to receive 20 to 25 solidi per year, some of the lower ranks only 10 to 15 solidi. And in the smallest centers, she points out, even the bishop would have had perhaps no more than 40 to 50 solidi, which would not have been an attractive income to someone of the upper classes.

At the lower end, let us imagine a reader (*anagnôstês*) who received 10 solidi per year. A complete Bible would cost him half a year's income. Such a purchase would have been entirely out of reach. Even an unbound short book, a single gospel on papyrus of the sort that cost a third of a solidus in the ostraka cited by Anne Boud'hors, would amount to one-thirtieth of a year's income—in proportionate terms (although not in purchasing power) the equivalent of $1,000 today, let us say, for someone earning $35,000. People at that sort of income level do not buy books at that price. Even the best-paid of academics do not buy many books at that price.

For a priest earning 25 solidi a year, a good income by ancient middle-class standards, a Bible would still have been a major expenditure, even if it was not a luxury version—almost like buying a small house, I suppose. A copy of the gospels alone would still have amounted to a large sum, but it was not unthinkable. It is not really until we get to the level of bishops that it is possible to imagine the regular buying of books as an affordable activity. Of course, a priest who had a large private income might have been able to afford more books from his own means, but we do not have enough evidence to say how common such wealth was among the priests, or even among bishops.

The figures I have been quoting are, of course, derived from sources of the sixth century or later. It is very unlikely that the church of the fourth century, far less institutionalized and endowed than the institution was two centuries later, had revenues on the same scale. We do encounter large numbers of clergy occasionally in the papyrological sources, but it is likely, as has often been pointed out, that they lived for the most part on income from landownings or other occupations; being a deacon or reader, at least, was not a full-time paid occupation at this period. If this was the case in the fourth century, we may suppose that it was even more true in the period before Constantine, when the churches were not yet recognized as legal persons able to own property.

Now it is not a new observation that ancient books were expensive relative to incomes. Sigrid Mratschek expressed it as follows: "The relationship between salaries and prices confirms the picture that books in the Byzantine period were an article beyond the financial means of a man with an average income" (2000: 373). That is not how I would put it. The man of average means was illiterate and had no need for books in any event. More importantly, books were apparently beyond the means even of a large part of those who were well above average in income. But even with that formulation, the implications bear some reflection.

First, books were not unique among the products of the artisan in being relatively expensive. Every papyrologist will have encountered prices for clothing and other products of weaving that seem relatively high. Even apart from some of the high-luxury goods we encounter, it was not unusual to have a chiton or mantle cost the equivalent of three or four artabas of wheat, several months' food for an adult. How could people afford to clothe themselves?

There are two explanations that in my opinion are the most probable, and they do not exclude one another. The first is that the papyrus documents, especially the private letters, that are our sources of information for these prices were mostly produced by the wealthy. This is a point that I have made on several occasions, most recently in the volume *Women's Letters from Ancient Egypt* that Raffaella Cribiore and I have written (Bagnall and Cribiore 2006). Papyrologists have generally assumed, much too easily, that we meet average people in the papyri, but this is surely untrue (briefly, Bagnall 1993: 5–6). It is therefore not surprising that we find people buying expensive clothing.

The second point is that it is a fundamental characteristic of preindustrial societies that the relationship of the cost of goods and of labor is very different from what we are accustomed to in a modern industrial society. Our expectation is that ordinary goods that we regard as necessities, like clothing, should be relatively inexpensive when compared with our incomes. This is largely true in modern developed societies. But this was not the case in antiquity, and it is not true in poorer countries today despite mass-produced imported goods. Things were expensive compared with incomes in antiquity, partly because most peoples' incomes were low and partly because virtually all the labor that went into making things was hand labor and not mechanized. Books required a lot of skilled labor, and their raw materials were also expensive. It was not until centuries later that the introduction of paper dramatically lowered the cost of writing material.[13]

Now I want to focus on the implications of these facts for the earliest period of Christian books—to return to a question I asked earlier about how many people were likely to have owned Christian books in the second, third, and beginning of the fourth centuries. How many Christian books should we expect to find?

As far as we have any good evidence, there were no organized monastic communities in Egypt before the time of Constantine (see above, p. 4, on the passage of Philo taken by Eusebius to refer to such). Institutional owners during this period could only have been the churches themselves, including any schools that were part of them. We know, of course, that a catechetical school existed in Alexandria,[14] but we know little about what was happening in the *chora*. The most likely situation, I believe, is that higher catechesis existed where there were bishops; that certainly is the impression that one gets from AnneMarie Luijendijk's (forthcoming) analysis of the group of letters from Sotas, perhaps a bishop in the third century. As we have seen, there were few such bishops before the second quarter of the third century. Of course the churches themselves must have had copies of at least the most essential scriptures for public reading, but it is difficult to say how much more they may have owned. As the hypothetical (but, I think, realistic) numbers I presented for Egyptian Christians show, the numbers of such churches did not become very large until after the middle of the third century.

Assessing the numbers of individually owned copies is more difficult. The few bishops may well have had their own collections of books, but their ability to do so must have depended principally on their personal wealth, because the church cannot at this time have had the revenues that made some bishops fairly wealthy at a later period. We do not have any direct information about the personal means of Egyptian bishops in the third century, as far as I am aware. The same may be said about priests of city or village churches. We have effectively no evidence about their typical level of wealth in the third century, and not much in the fourth.

When we turn to think about individual Christians who were not members of the clergy, we are more or less entirely without direct information. How many of them, few as they were until well into the third century, were wealthy enough to buy books? Unless the early Christians were drawn disproportionately from the uppermost stratum of society, the answer must be that very few were. Although modern scholars of early Christianity have offered different opinions about the social origins of Christians, probably the highest estimate that could be defended would be that Christians were in many cases socially and economically mobile, not of the social elite but perhaps some of them of an economic level just below the elite and lacking the social role that their wealth would have entitled them to had it not been recently acquired.[15] It is certainly not impossible to imagine that some of these people could have bought books. But their numbers cannot have been large in the second century. This observation, coupled with the weak institutional base of the Egyptian church in the second century, only reinforces the point that I have been urging from the beginning of this book, that the inherent probability of finding many Christian books truly datable to the second century is very low.

I shall turn now to a different approach in thinking about the period at the end of the second century and the start of the third, the period when Demetrios was bishop of Alexandria. It is obvious that we have a considerable number of books or fragments of books from this period. Even if some of those dated to the early third century should in fact be attributed to later in that century, it can hardly be denied that a significant number remain that probably belong to the first quarter of the third century. Most of these probably come from nome capitals, many of course from Oxyrhynchus, others from a variety of other provenances, but strikingly few from the Fayyum. Because the sources of Fayyum papyri in the second and third century are almost entirely villages, we have a kind of confirmation that Christian books in Egypt outside Alexandria were found almost entirely in the cities. That is not surprising, of course, but it is worth emphasizing.

Despite all the external reasons why there should not be many books, even from the third century, then, there is a fair number of them from the third century. If we had papyri from Alexandria, of course, we might expect this. Clearly there was a group of well-educated Alexandrian Christians in the late second century. It need not have been very large, but Clement and Origen cannot have been figures in complete isolation, either. People with a good classical education certainly came from families with the means to have afforded books.[16] But it is less obvious that there would have been such people in the other cities of Egypt.

I would like next to look at this question from another point of view altogether. Chester Beatty Papyrus VII, a codex of Isaiah of which fragments are also kept in Florence and the Merton collection (LDAB 3108), was dated by Frederic Kenyon to the third century, and probably to its first half. It is distinctive among the other Christian codices of this period in its marginal glosses in Coptic. These are in many cases difficult to understand. Walter Crum's words about them should cause even the boldest of us to tremble: "But in so many cases the reading I have proposed is anything but reliable, is indeed often obviously valueless, that bases for general conclusions are inadequate." He does, however, make several crucial observations. One is that the dialect of the glosses is entirely Fayyumic. The second is that these glosses, although genuinely Coptic in linguistic terms, are entirely lacking in the supplementary letters derived from Demotic that characterize developed Coptic script. The third is that he thinks the glosses were written "not long after the writing of the Greek text." He gives no basis for this last opinion, but one must imagine that it is palaeographically based.

What are these glosses doing in the margin, and what can they tell us about the audience for Greek copies of Christian scriptures in the third century? First, I should note that the Coptic hand is faster than the book-hand of the manuscript and must be described as practiced. This was a highly experienced writer. Second, this is probably the earliest text that might be called truly Coptic. Its predecessors in the development of the writing of Egyptian in Greek letters come from a temple milieu and never include Greek vocabulary. These are what is usually called Old Coptic.[17] The remarkable ostrakon from Kellis that has supplemental letters but not yet in their definitive and standardized form, which Iain Gardner, the editor, called Old Coptic, is in my view better called something else; it is Coptic, even if one might want to call it "early Coptic" or "formative Coptic." It is obviously from a later stage of development than the Beatty glosses, although not probably in the same line of development. It is probably to be dated to the second half of the third century, perhaps to its third quarter, although the archaeological context cannot be pinned down with great precision. An earlier date for the glosses would agree with Crum's judgment that the date was not much after the writing of the Greek that Kenyon put in the first part of the third century. We might say that they were from the middle of the third century, with a significant margin on either side of that date. Importantly, they do use Greek words; in fact, in some instances the Greek word is the word used in the Greek text (as in f. 86v).

Our glossator thus is a member of the book-possessing population, bilingual, a fluent writer, from the Fayyum or somewhere in its vicinity, and probably something of an experimenter with language, because he is not working in an established writing system that he could have learned in school or anywhere else. And, of course, he may be assumed to be a Christian.

In a more speculative vein, I would go further and suggest that he was a member of that urban elite formed in the aftermath of the creation of the city councils of the metropoleis of the nomes after 200. We still know relatively little about the formation of this elite, but I am reminded of the case that Peter van Minnen made for identifying *P.Amst.* 72 as a list of names that included a number of persons with Egyptian names who had taken Greek names, often calques of the Egyptian names, in the wake of the Severan creation of the councils (van Minnen 1986; cf. Bagnall 1995: 36–37). These hellenized

Egyptians participating in the institutionalized civic life of the third century have long seemed to me the most likely milieu for the development of a distinctively Christian Coptic writing system, and the owner of *P.Chester Beatty* VII could well be someone of this sort. He would have been well off financially, well educated, and bilingual; at the same time, his education was probably Greek rather than priestly Egyptian, and he was very much aware of the potential of the Greek alphabet to be a bearer of the Egyptian language at a point when Demotic had long ceased to be a viable script in daily life.[18]

Anyone familiar with the literature on early Christianity will probably be reminded of the influential book *The First Urban Christians*, published in 1983 by Wayne Meeks. Writing about the people whom we can observe in the social world of the Pauline letters, Meeks said, "We found that their dominant characteristic was status inconsistency or social mobility." He went on to speculate, "May we further guess that the sorts of status inconsistency we observed—independent women with moderate wealth, Jews with wealth in a pagan society, freedmen with skill and money but stigmatized by origin, and so on—brought with them not only anxiety but also loneliness, in a society in which social position was important and usually rigid?" (Meeks 1983: 191).

It does not seem to me unreasonable to think that the process of recruiting city councils produced some of the same social dynamics in Egypt. We know nothing about it directly, but if van Minnen's explanation of the Amsterdam papyrus is even close to correct, it suggests that when the metropoleis became cities with councils under Septimius Severus, it was not a simple matter to supply them all with suitable governing classes. If all the members were to come from those defined as official Hellenes in the Roman system—legally speaking Egyptians, of course, but with preferential poll-tax rates and gymnasium membership among the markers of a higher status—it might not have been simple to find enough with the financial means to be councillors. I rather suspect that a desire for Hellenic ancestry collided with the need for a solvent governing class, and inevitably some of the slots were filled by hellenized Egyptians. These might take on the protective coloration of Greek names, but in my hypothesis they were far from having discarded entirely their Egyptian identity, particularly in language. This was probably the most bilingual part of Egyptian society. But the social dynamics described by Meeks could well have come into play; these men were not in fact Greeks in the eyes of the small elite of ethnic Greeks who were also rich enough to make it into the councils, and I am sure that they were aware of this.

Despite the speculative character of the foregoing, we have here at least the beginnings of a hypothesis about how a body of Greek-reading, educated, well-to-do, book-owning Christians could have come into being and how the leadership of the church might already in the first half of the third century have been interested in developing a form of Egyptian that would serve the needs of their religion. We might also see here the reason why we have so many Christian books from the third century, surely more than the raw numbers of Christians or the nature of the educational system would lead us to expect, as I have argued earlier. We have thus a possible explanation for how these books could have been created in a world largely devoid of well-financed church institutions. It may not be the correct explanation—I am very well aware of how speculative it is. But at least it would help us to understand how an artifact as expensive as the book could come to exist in significant numbers in the service of a religion that otherwise had, as far as we can see, no particular grip on the only class in the society with the financial means to purchase or commission such a luxury.

CHAPTER IV

The Spread of the Codex

Even if readers of this book have charitably accorded me a high level of indulgence so far in my explorations of well-known territory concerning early Christian books in Egypt, they may be wondering if there really is anything new of any value to be said about the origins and spread of the codex. What I would say at the outset is that some of the same problems of expectations, agendas, and tendentious arguments that have made the other subjects I have discussed so problematic are with us here as well, and I think that there is something to be learned by looking at them closely. I think also that it is possible to be more precise about some of the patterns we see.

Probably I should have begun this book by defining the phrase "Christian books," which I used in the title. But nothing of importance rested on a definition until now, because in the first two chapters I was dealing with very defined groups of biblical or near-biblical texts, and in the third with questions that affect Christian and non-Christian books alike. In discussing the codex, however, it is important to be clear about what will or will not be included as "Christian." In this context I am using the phrase as a kind of shorthand[1] for books containing works of a specifically Christian character. There were of course many books owned by Christians that do not fall into this category, like the codex of Menander owned by Dioskoros of Aphrodito. There were also books composed by Christians that do not fall into this category, like the *Kestoi* of Julius Africanus (which the Leuven Database of Ancient Books categorizes as religion = Christian) or the

Dionysiaka of Nonnos of Panopolis, whose paraphrase of the Gospel of John *would* be included in the category.

Most of the Christian books, in this sense, that we have were produced in the form of a codex, that is, rectangular leaves of papyrus or parchment folded into a notebook, usually stitched in some fashion along the spine, and sometimes given an outer binding. A generation ago, no one except a papyrologist would have thought a book could be anything else, because the codex is nothing other than the traditional book that for more than 1,500 years has been the characteristic form in which Mediterranean and European societies have disseminated written works of any length. Today, the electronic book, although still in a sense in its infancy, has become ubiquitous enough that we may confidently look to the day when "book" by itself will not normally and necessarily mean the traditional book and when we will have to specify a printed book in codex form if that is what we mean.

In the ancient world, as is well known, the concept of the book, and particularly of the book containing literature, was different from the codex. The normal book was, still in the third century, the book roll. The transition from the roll to the codex as the normal book-form is one of the major technological changes of the Roman world and has therefore received much attention from scholars over the years. But this gradual passage from one form of the book to another was a social and cultural transformation, not merely a technological one, for the forms of books embed cultural practices.[2]

One cultural dimension of this change is the persistent association of the codex with Christianity. There has been much controversy about this point, and there have been many attempts to claim Christian parentage for the codex. Today, most careful scholars acknowledge that Christianity is in no way connected with the *origins* of the codex as a book-form (e.g., Emmel 1998). But even so, in virtually every treatment of the subject we can read that Christians preferred the codex to the roll, to a degree not true of non-Christians in the first four centuries of our era (most recently, Hurtado 2006: 5–6). In this way, a distinctive association between Christianity and the codex remains part of our picture of the history of the book.

In reality, such statements are partly misleading and need significant qualification.[3] I shall try to set the facts out as briefly and clearly as I can.

Some numbers are going to be unavoidable, but I will present them in tabular form in the hope that they will not be too difficult to follow. It will become evident, along the way, why I have been so concerned with the dating of manuscripts in the first two chapters. Many dates based on palaeography remain unavoidably vague, even with the best of scholarly attention. To avoid the risk of circular argument, I am for the moment going to use the most generally accepted dates for the pieces I cite. The data have been compiled from the Leuven Database of Ancient Books, which has the advantage of being more or less up-to-date and possesses the characteristic—for better or worse—of not embodying any single idiosyncratic viewpoint about the dating of manuscripts. This has, at least at this stage in the argument, the advantage over trying to redate these manuscripts myself or seeming to slant the argument by using the sometimes later dates by Turner and others that I mentioned in chapter 1. But I shall also tabulate some dates according to Turner to show that the basic points at stake are not changed by doing so.

Table 4.1 shows the numbers of codices from Egypt dated to the first four centuries of the Christian era; those assigned dates spanning centuries, as in "II/III" (second to third), are displayed in separate columns to show the direction of development as clearly and precisely as possible.

The numbers dated to the earlier centuries are of course modest, and even some of these may, as we have seen, be dated too early. We must also keep in mind the effects to be expected from the rapid growth in numbers of Christians from the middle of the third cen-

TABLE 4.1
Christian and Non-Christian Codices by Century (LDAB datings)

Century	I	I/II	II	II/III	III	III/IV	IV
Total codices	3	3	27	67	186	124	252
Non-Christian codices	3	2	21	47	123	80	153
Christian codices	0	1	6	20	63	44	99
Christian as percentage of the total	0	33	22	30	34	35	39

tury onward, as well as the impact of the official Christianization of the empire beginning in the time of Constantine. We should thus in any event expect some rise in the percentage of the total made up of Christian texts in the late third and even more in the fourth century, and we do have such a rise. It is striking, however, that even in the fourth century classical literature and other types of non-Christian text make up something like three-fifths of the population of codices, and before that point non-Christian texts make up an even higher percentage of codices. This is part of the reason that it has become impossible to maintain that the codex was a specifically Christian book-form or that the move from roll to codex in the Roman world was primarily driven by Christianity.

By way of comparison, as promised, I provide a similar table derived from the work of Eric Turner published nearly three decades ago, thus with less evidence available but with a single viewpoint about dating imposed on the evidence (see table 4.2).

It is striking, comparing the tables, to notice that although Turner had less material available to him and dated many codices later than their editors and other scholars have done, the overall percentage pattern is not very much different. The Christian percentage from the end of the third century rises somewhat more than with the Leuven Database datings; that is all. It is thus likely that no amount of scholarly difference over the dating of individual manuscripts would change the general picture, although clearly there are important questions still to be considered about the very earliest examples of the codex.

TABLE 4.2
Christian and Non-Christian Codices by Century (Datings by E. G. Turner)

Century	I	I/II	II	II/III	III	III/IV
Total codices	0	0	17	23	140	58
Non-Christian codices	0	0	12	16	91	33
Christian codices	0	0	5	7	49	25
Christian as percentage	0	0	29.4	30.4	35	43

It is, however, true that Christian books in these centuries are far more likely to be codices than rolls, quite the reverse of what we find with classical literature. Even here, however, the picture is more interesting than one is often led to believe. Almost all texts that can be described as scripture appear in codex form. In this category I include the Old Testament, which was effectively canonical for Christians of this period; the books of the New Testament, although not yet fully canonized; those gospels that did not make it into the eventual canon, like Thomas; and the *Shepherd* by Hermas, a very popular also-ran (see chapter 2).[4] Up to the turn of the second to third centuries, the twenty-seven Christian (or probably Christian) codices shown in table 4.1 consist entirely of scripture in this sense, as far as the texts have been identified.[5] By contrast, there are 9 or 10 Christian texts in roll form, of which only three might be scripture. Table 4.3 lists all 10.

At first glance, it seems that five of these are biblical. But a closer look is warranted. Of these biblical texts (as before, including apocryphal gospels and the like), one (*P.Oxy.* XLI 2949) is very fragmentary, and even its identification as a roll is by no means certain, as it is a

TABLE 4.3
Early Christian Manuscripts in Roll Form

Century	LDAB	Reference	Contents
I/II	4443	*P.Oxy.* LXV 4443	Esther, 3 cols.
II	3082	Roca-Puig	Psalm
II	4669	*PSI* XI 1200 bis	Patristic text
II/III	562	*P.Mich.* XVIII 764	Clement? letter or homily
II/III	2459	*P.Oxy.* III 405	Irenaeus
II/III	2776	*P.IFAO* II 31	Revelation; on verso
II/III	3088	*PSI* VIII 821 v	Psalm; on verso
II/III	5071	*P.Mich.* XVIII 763	letter or homily; on verso
II/III	5111	*P.Oxy.* XLI 2949	apocryphal gospel
II/III	10575	*P.Oxy.* LXIX 4706	Hermas

Figure 4.1. *P.Oxy.* XLI 2949.
Photo courtesy of the Egypt
Exploration Society.

small fragment of an unknown text, presumably an apocryphal gospel, concerning Joseph of Arimathaia's request to Pilate for Jesus's body for burial (figure 4.1). The editor suggested that it was from a roll only because the back is blank; but it is by no means impossible that the text ended not long after the surviving fragment, as for example the Gospel of Mark does, and in that case it could come from the end of a codex. LDAB 3082 is also not certainly from a roll; it is not excluded that it could be a copy of one psalm on a separate sheet. A third biblical text, Esther (*P.Oxy.* LXV 4443), is not clearly Christian; there is nothing to prevent it from being Jewish, and at the date assigned to it there was still a thriving Jewish community in Egypt.

FIGURE 4.2. PSI VIII 921. Photo courtesy Graeco-Roman Museum, Alexandria.

The remaining two possibly biblical texts are copies of scripture made on the backs of obsolete documentary texts, the Psalms on the back of a register dating to 143/144 (*PSI* VIII 921) (figure 4.2) and the Apocalypse of John on the back of an unidentified document (*P.IFAO* II 31) (figure 4.3).[6] In sum, when making private copies on used papyrus, early Christians behaved just like anyone else, using the blank backs, but otherwise, when not recycling, they put scripture into codices but homilies and the like into book rolls, as if they were normal literary texts. The codex was thus not so much adopted generally by

FIGURE 4.3. *P.IFAO* II 31. Photo reproduced with permission of the Institut français d'archéologie orientale, Cairo.

the early Christians for their book production; rather, the Christians adopted the codex as the normative format of deliberately produced public copies of scriptural texts,[7] but they did not generalize from this adoption to broader use for all books. Or at least they did not do so a great deal sooner than other people did.

Hermas occupies a peculiar and interesting position in the schematic dichotomy that I am proposing. Of the three apparently earliest texts of parts of the *Shepherd*, dated to the second to third century, two are from codices and one from a roll, which does not have a text on the other side—that is, it is a proper book rather than a private reuse. In chapter 2, I described the difficulties involved in being certain about the date to be assigned to *P.Iand.* 4, a codex fragment perhaps as early as the middle of the second century.

When we come to texts dated simply to the third century, the situation remains similar but with some interesting details. Table 4.4 is a simple presentation of the numbers of codices and rolls by category of content.

The scanty numbers for the canonical and near-canonical biblical books in roll form are less impressive than they may appear. One of the Old Testament papyri (LDAB 3104) may be Jewish; another (LDAB 3117) is a fragment of uncertain nature with a quotation from Isaiah. Both of the New Testament papyri are written on the ver-

TABLE 4.4
Third-Century Christian Texts

Category	Codices	Rolls
Old Testament	23	3
New Testament	27	2
Apocryphal biblical	3	6
Hermas	4	2
Patristic	6	2
Other	3	4
Total	66	19

sos of rolls, like earlier cases we have seen; so are one of the texts of the Gospel of Thomas and both of the roll-form copies of Hermas. In texts other than the Old and New Testaments, however, codices barely outnumber rolls; in full copies of the scriptures, the codex is absolutely standard.[8]

The same sort of analysis deployed so far in talking about the choice of codex or roll may also be applied to the other great innovation in book production in the early Roman centuries, the use of parchment as the material for the leaves. If we look at the parchment books in codex form known from Egypt from the period up through the fourth century, we find a total of 131, of which 48, or 36.3 percent, are Christian. This percentage does not differ materially from the Christian percentage of all codices. That is, parchment like the codex is used irrespective of religion. The use of parchment is not a sign of Christianity, but it is perhaps strongly connected to the codex.[9] As time went on and the codex became virtually the only possible format for books, parchment retained a distinctive place in the ecosystem of book production. As Edoardo Crisci has shown, it was used above all and dominantly for good-quality copies of the scriptures, no doubt made for institutional use, while papyrus continued to dominate in works other than scripture (2003: 104–5). The analysis of the cost of book production in chapter 3 showed just how dramatic the cost difference between papyrus and parchment was. The choice between them was not a neutral one, in which taste or ideology alone would make the decision. It was a choice between ordinary and luxurious.

But even if all this is agreed on, we are still stuck with the obvious question: Why did the Christians use the codex format for scripture? The usage of the codex for this purpose, and in the early stages only this purpose, is so uniform, apart from private copying, that we cannot even describe it as merely a tendency. It is a rule. Although the Christians may not have used the codex for other types of written material significantly earlier or to a much greater degree than other people, they did apparently adopt it from as early a date as we have evidence as the standard format for professional copies of the Bible.

In general, recent scholarship has offered one of three possible explanations. One of them, argued most extensively by the late Colin

Roberts and Theodore Skeat, is that the codex was adopted because it was the only book-form that was capable of holding all four of the canonical gospels in a single unit.[10] A second proposal, like Roberts and Skeat's except for the identity of the works alleged as the grounds, was argued by Harry Gamble, who proposed that the Pauline corpus of letters was the candidate that made the codex attractive by virtue of its capability of holding the entire corpus (Gamble 1995: 62–66). A third direction of inquiry, more suggested than argued, is that because many of the external characteristics of the early Christian book come from Judaism and reflect the Jewish character of early Christianity, so also might the codex. This is a position deriving from ideas of Kurt Treu (1973/1991; cf. above, p. 24) and explored in recent years by Robert Kraft, who in one paper said, "While hard evidence has not yet surfaced to connect this [the codex] as well to Greek Judaism, the possible pattern of continuity between Greek Jewish scribal practices and early Christian texts suggests that the possibility should not be ignored that codex technology was also part of the heritage early Christian copyists adapted from their Jewish predecessors."[11]

Because this position has not yet, as far as I know, been argued fully in print, it is impossible to respond to it in the same fashion that one can to the other dominant theories. Whatever the possibilities, however, that Christians may have adopted some external characteristics of the book from Jewish scribal practice, there is, as Kraft admits, not a shred of evidence that the use of the codex came from Judaism, for the simple reason that the surviving fragments of possibly Jewish codices come from a period no earlier than the period (late second century) from which also come most of our early Christian codex fragments. Indeed, the use of the roll for scripture has sometimes been taken by scholars as evidence that the papyrus or parchment in question is Jewish rather than Christian, a point that obviously comes into play in considering the Oxyrhynchus copy of Esther that I mentioned earlier.[12] In any case, nothing in the view of the diffusion of the codex argued here, which de-emphasizes any specifically Christian character of the codex, would be affected by the presence of some Jewish codices.

The other two of these proposals seem to me doubtful on a priori grounds: They rely too much on coincidence and invite the invention of contrafactual hypotheses: Would the Christians have used the book roll for the gospels if there had been only three of them? Or for Paul's letters if there had been only half as many of them? Indeed, I find the entire idea that the choice of the form of a book was driven by the volume of material to be included in it very odd, an extreme kind of special pleading. Would such an argument be used if anything other than Christianity was at stake? Even later, when Christianity was far better established, the gospels often were produced as separate codices rather than put together in a single codex. Why would the desire to assemble them in a single unit have led to something so far-reaching and apparently radical as a uniform rule in favor of the codex?

There is another major difficulty in both of these hypotheses, too. At least in the case of the gospels, and perhaps also with the Pauline letters, they also depend to some degree on an early date for the emergence of a Christian sense of canonicity. In other words, these hypotheses require Christians to have fastened on precisely the four-gospel canon and the accepted list of the Pauline letters almost as early as the ink was drying on the autograph of John, the later pastoral epistles (attributed to Paul but generally not regarded today as being his), or the Apocalypse of John. The fact that gospels that did not make it into the eventual canon and authors like Hermas who also did not make the cut are written in the form of the codex almost as much as Matthew, Luke, John, and Paul, and that the use of the codex for these noncanonical texts is strongest in the earliest manuscripts, suggests that any confidence in an emerging canon as the basis of the use of the codex is misplaced. It was not a specific canon but a type of material that the church—I leave aside for the present the question of exactly who "the church" is—decided to reproduce in codex form.[13]

The adoption of the codex was certainly not a minor matter, a choice that could easily have gone either way. It implies a radical shift in the way the book was thought of. That is why all the explanations based solely on convenience seem to me unsatisfying. That a significant cultural change was at stake emerges from the work of William Johnson, who has shown that there is a close relationship between the format of the elegant Greek book roll and the cognitive process by which these rolls were used. The typical column of writing, at 4.5

to 7 cm or 15–25 letters wide, is the maximum that the eye is capable of taking in at a singular ocular fixation and processing before moving on to a new point. That is, one reads a single line of a column as a unit. Johnson argues that this process is linked to the normal use of such rolls for performative oral reading in elite circles.

The codex, although coming in a considerable variety of formats, involves in almost all cases a considerably wider horizontal span of writing in a column than does the roll, except in the minority of codices where the narrow column format is borrowed from the book roll to present two columns (or occasionally even more). That is, the reader of the codex could not normally have taken in the entire width of the page, typically between three and four times as wide as with a book-roll column, at a glance.[14] That is true even though some codices, particularly Christian, feature larger letter sizes and thus would probably have been read from a somewhat greater distance, opening up a wider ocular span. Some of the early non-Christian codices are indeed of works unlikely to have been read aloud in the manner Johnson describes—a Homeric lexicon, medical works, hypotheses, astronomical tables, and the like. Others, however, are of standard classical authors.

If it is true, as Johnson says, that the juncture of narrow columns, *scriptio continua* (that is, the lack of division between words and sentences), and elite performative reading had successfully formed a system of reading for hundreds of years, what could have caused it to be perceived as inadequate by at least some readers, so that it was progressively replaced by a very different system, one that kept *scriptio continua* but did not adopt the rest of the system in which it was embedded?

Two elements in the system seem possible candidates for having been destabilized by the early Roman imperial period. One of them is the elite character of reading. Johnson (2000: 615) says, "that reading was largely an elitist phenomenon was accepted as a matter of course." This is in my view a misdescription of the situation. The kind of literary reading he is discussing may well have been so, but reading was in fact an everyday activity for a much wider range of people. In any case, although the matter can hardly be argued here, I think that reading and writing were accessible to wider circles in the imperial period than they had been before.[15] That does not mean that the elite ceased to engage in the kind of usage that Johnson describes; after all, the book roll with its narrow columns continued to rule the book trade for a couple of centuries, and some of Johnson's most telling anecdotal evidence comes from the first two centuries of the empire.

The second, and connected, possibility is that the performative character of reading became less relevant to the range of material finding expression in book form in the imperial period. That is not to say, of course, that performance ceased to be important in the texts of this period—far from it. Rhetoric, in particular, flourished. But that is a different matter from reading books.

We should turn at this point to explore some critical aspects of the question of how changes in the contents of books and the ways in which they were read may have influenced the shift from roll to codex. A rare opportunity to do this in something like a controlled experiment is offered by the so-called Theban magical library. This body of material, which includes many of the most famous magical papyri, was acquired in the nineteenth century by European museums and libraries, a large part of it coming from the nineteenth-century acquisitions in Upper Egypt of a single individual, and possibly all from a single find in a tomb in the West Bank at Thebes. But the individual in question, Giovanni Anastasy, left no records that allow us to be certain that the papyri in question actually form a single trove, and modern opinion has been divided on the question. Table 4.5 shows the composition of the Theban "library" in the view of the most recent serious study, that of Jacco Dieleman. In the top part are the items he considers to be attributed to the find with certainty, in the bottom part those of which the attribution is not certain.

A number of points are immediately obvious in this tabular presentation. First, the items usually regarded as being certainly part of the library are mostly in codex form and entirely in Greek, except for some passages in an early form of Coptic in *PGM* IV. They are to be assigned to the fourth century or at the earliest the very end of the third century, without much doubt. By contrast, the items about which doubt has been expressed are all in roll form, and all, in my view, belong to the third century. It is only fair to say that some of

TABLE 4.5
The Theban Magical Library

Reference	Description	Languages*	Form	Date	Notes
PGM IV = Suppl.Gr. 574	Magical handbook	G, C	codex	IV	
PGM V = P.Lond. I 46	Magical handbook	G	codex	IV	
PGM Va	Magical spell	G	sheet	IV	hand A
P.Leid. J397	Alchemical handbook	G	codex	IV	hand A
P.Holm.	Alchemical handbook	G	codex	IV	hand A
PGM XII = P.Leid. J395	Magical handbook	G	codex	IV	
PGM XII = P.Leid. J384	Magical handbook	D, G	roll	ca 200–225	hand B. On verso of Demotic literary text
PGM XIV = P.Leid. J383 + P.BM 10070	Magical handbook	D, G	roll	ca 200–225	hand B
PGM III = P.Louvre 2391	Magical handbook	G, C	roll	III	
PGM I = P.Berl. 5025	Magical handbook	G	roll	III	
PGM II = P.Berl. 5026	Magical handbook	G	roll	III	
PGM VII = P.Lond. 121	Magical handbook	G	roll	III early	
PGM LXI = P.BM 10588	Magical handbook	D, G, OC	roll	III	
PDM Suppl. = P.Louvre 3229	Magical handbook	H, D, OC	roll	III	G on verso erased

* C = Coptic; D = Demotic; G = Greek; H = Hieratic; OC = Old Coptic

these have been dated later by other scholars. But these dates have rested on no solid foundation of comparison with datable handwritings and have, I think, proceeded from a priori assumptions about a date for the entire library in the fourth century. Dieleman has shown, conclusively in my view, that the two rolls assigned "certainly" to the group do not belong to the fourth century but to the first quarter of the third century.[16]

It would be surprising if some readers, looking at table 4.5, did not ask whether the two rolls in the "certain" group really deserve to be listed there, or whether the unity of the "Theban Magical Library" should be called into question. The major basis for positing the unity of the "certain" group is the fact that the four pieces in Leiden were all sold to the Rijksmuseum van Oudheden by Anastasy as a group in 1828. It is therefore supposed that he acquired them together. The Leiden purchase includes two codices and two rolls, and the two rolls show the handwriting of the same scribe. Of course we know nothing of the circumstances of the finding of this material, and Anastasy could perfectly well have combined material from two finds, two tombs let us say, for purposes of marketing.

But that hypothesis is not any more economical than supposing that in fact all, or virtually all, of the texts do belong to the same find. In that case, one would be faced with a trove containing texts with dates spread over a considerable period. But that is not in itself an impossibility. One of the Leiden texts, as we have noted, was written on the back of a roll with a literary work in Demotic that has been assigned to a period several centuries earlier. A practitioner of magic could well have treasured the old rolls he had managed to obtain, through inheritance or purchase, and have kept them with the newer books he had written, or had caused to be written, in his own time. In that event, the Theban Magical Library becomes a kind of cross section of book-forms in use for capturing magical spells and other material during the third and fourth centuries. The dividing point, very approximately, would seem to be the very late third or very early fourth century. Before that point, everything is in roll form; after that, everything is in codex form. Or, perhaps, our magician's inheritance was in roll form, but his recent acquisitions were in codex form.

Magical handbooks were not literature; they did not come to the use of the book-roll form through direct inheritance from the Greek book trade. Rather, the magical rolls were products of the temples, and they owe their form to the habits of Egyptian scribes, who were accustomed to using rolls long before the Greeks learned to write. The temples never made the transition from roll to codex, although they obviously did begin in the course of the Roman period to use Greek alongside Demotic and hieratic. The shift in the magical texts from roll to codex marks not only the passage of time but also the privatization of magic, the acquisition of the books by an individual or family, and the entry of treatises on magic into the world of the Greek book.

Another critical point where the Theban magical texts may help our inquiry is that it is hard to suppose that those responsible for them switched from roll to codex because of the influence of Christianity. The change comes too early for Christianity to be exerting the kind of dominant influence that this would require, and it would require some gymnastics to think of these codices as Christian in any way—although that tells us nothing about the religious identity of their possessors.

The Theban Magical Library thus helps to confirm the sense that the significant numbers of non-Christian codices before the late third or early fourth century already gave us, that Christian influence cannot really be offered as an explanation for the spread of the codex, even as late as the period just before Constantine.

In thinking about how the codex came to be used for books, and indeed to be used widely for books, the nature of the contents of the early non-Christian codices has already been seen to be significant. Another aspect of the contents is connected to the fact that the codex is an artifact of Roman civilization. Many authors have in fact noticed that the case for the Roman origin of the codex is strong, even decisive.[17] Our first good evidence of its use for books (as opposed to private notes and memoranda, written on wooden tablets strung together) comes from first-century Rome. The origin of the codex in such groups of tablets strung together is now, I believe, generally admitted. What is perhaps not quite so generally appreciated is just how deeply rooted in Roman culture the use of tablets was. A recent book by Elizabeth Meyer (2004) has now given us a profoundly insightful and detailed picture of the history, social place, and ideological function of tablets as repositories of authoritative and trustworthy information, whether in legal documents or in personal or official records. In the first century of our era they were in very widespread use, and the combination of two and three of them together became common. A *Senatus consultum* of 61 CE regulated their use and shows what official importance was attached to them by the elite. As time went on, their use around the empire grew, largely a mark of a choice by local elites to adopt Roman ways.

Given the Roman character of tablets and the near-certainty that the codex originated at Rome from an adaptation of the codex of tablets, it seems logical to suggest that the wider, if gradual, adoption of the codex elsewhere is yet another manifestation of what for short we may still call Romanization, the spread of Roman habits and technologies throughout the empire. This is surely far more plausible than the other hypotheses that I have just dismissed. This was, indeed, the explanation for the adoption of the codex for documentary purposes in fourth-century Egypt offered by Jean Gascou (1989: 75–77) twenty years ago. It is just as likely to be correct for the adoption of the codex for books.

Indeed, what is most odd, and perhaps symptomatic of the state of early Christian studies, is that scholars have been unwilling or unable to make the logical move from the widely observed fact of the Roman origin of the codex to the idea that the dissemination of this book-form is also Roman. Perhaps part of the cause is an underlying and unanalyzed discomfort with the idea that the Christian church, so commonly thought of in this period as a kind of countercultural movement unfriendly to the imperial power, would have fastened on an artifact specifically associated with the Roman elite and mandated its use for its most central treasury of text. But surely the alternative path open to the early church would not have been preferable; this would be, in effect, to identify the scriptures with Greek elite literature by adopting the technology of that literature.[18] Indeed, the earliest "codex" books in Egypt that are not Christian are also not bearers of Greek literature in book form.[19] One is in fact made of waxed tablets inscribed with poems of Poseidippos (LDAB 3850);

another comes from an astrological manual (LDAB 4293);[20] a third is an unknown Latin historical text on parchment (LDAB 4472; *P.Oxy.* I 30); these are the only three items that have been dated by any reputable scholar to the first century or the turn of the first to second. Only when we reach the second century do we begin to find true books of Greek literature in codex form, and not many of these. Of the thirteen codices classified by the Leuven Database under the rubric codices of classical culture (actually, of classical "religion" according to the database) produced in the second century, two are wooden tablets (and thus scholastic, 2642, 7990); five are manuals of various types (astrology [4771], lexica [296, 1515], grammar [7989], medicine [4934]); and one contains music (4867). Only five are literary by a strict definition: Pindar (3711), Plato (3790), Menander (2648), hexameters of an unknown author (4871), and Lollianus (2577).

I recognize that my suggestion that we look to Romanization can be no more than a hypothesis. But in general I believe that the combination of the use of the Greek language for the scriptures, the location of almost all the narrative of the early church's life in the Greek East, and the fact that it was the Roman authorities who crucified Jesus has tended to lead modern scholarship to structure inquiry into the world of early Christianity too much in a Greek framework and too little in a Roman mold. *Ex oriente lux* has been taken too seriously. The codex may be one of the signs of just how Roman the world of early Christianity was.

There may be a trace of this link visible in the tendency for Latin books in Egypt to be in codex form. Where Greek books—across the full span of the first four centuries CE—use the roll over the codex by a ratio of almost two to one, three-quarters of all Latin books from Egypt are codices. We should not push these numbers too far, because the Latin codices are mostly late, and the pattern may be explainable largely by chronology, but at least it seems possible to say that there is an association between adoption of the codex and the spread of the use of Latin.

This pattern of adoption throws into higher relief the early Christian adoption of the codex for scripture. Even if, as I have argued in earlier chapters, some of the dates proposed for Christian biblical papyrus manuscripts are too early, there is no doubt at all that the church routinely and uniformly used the codex for scripture in the period from the end of the second to the beginning of the third century, when it becomes visible as an institutional presence in Egypt. That is a century before society at large seems to have reached even the point of moderately widespread use of the codex, and it highlights the distinctiveness and specificity of Christian practice. It is in this sense that we may still consider that the codex has an association with Christianity.

I realize that I have not offered so much an explanation of the adoption of the codex for Christian scriptures as a description of the cultural milieu in which this adoption took place.[21] It is worth bearing in mind what Larry Hurtado has called the semiotic nature of the adoption of the codex—that is, as I have argued above, that it is a matter of cultural significance and not merely a question of convenience. Again, it does not seem to me that the various views that see an evolutionary character in the change take adequate account of the uniformity of practice that we see in the matter of the scriptures. The alert reader will realize that we are headed back in the direction of the view put forward by Roberts and Skeat that the adoption must derive from a center with "sufficient authority to devise such innovations and to impose them on Christendom generally."[22] They suggested Jerusalem and Antioch as possibilities. Few scholars have been persuaded, and Hurtado has argued that the proposal "naively assumes a scheme of ecclesiastical authority and centralization that is seriously anachronistic for the first and early second centuries CE." Skeat, Hurtado points out (2006: 72 n. 95), later came to think that it was the Roman church that played the decisive role (Skeat 1994).

That suggestion, of course, is equally vulnerable to the objection against early centralization just quoted. But that objection itself rests tacitly on the conviction that the earliest Christian books known from Egypt go back to the beginning of the second century. Supposing they do not? As we have seen in chapter 1, we can be sure of nothing before the middle of the second century, and not much before its close. If we were to accept the dating of *P.Ryl.* 457 to the late second century and see *P.Iand.* 4 as a case of archaism or incompetence, would the codex really need to have been adopted sooner than the middle of the second century? And at that point, would such a culturally determining role for the church of Rome really be unthinkable?[23] I do not know the answers to these questions, but they deserve to be taken seriously, and they show us just how weak are the foundations underlying much of the debate over the origins of the codex.

Notes

PREFACE

[1] For a survey of the Christian presence in both literary and documentary texts, the reader will find not only Hurtado 2006 but Choat 2006 valuable for up-to-date synthesis and bibliography. S. F. Johnson, *Bryn Mawr Classical Review* 2007.06.41, has noted that the title of Grafton and Williams 2006 (*Christianity and the Transformation of the Book*) "appears somewhat overstated."

CHAPTER I. THE DATING OF THE EARLIEST CHRISTIAN BOOKS IN EGYPT

[1] For a good introduction, see Ehrman 2003.

[2] Harnack 1908/1962: 369–80 already emphasized this characteristic of the early churches.

[3] It is an interesting exercise to search a major library catalogue for titles containing "Christian" and "origins." Even with date limits there are hundreds of hits.

[4] See Kasser, Meyer, and Wurst 2006 for a translation, and Krosney 2006 for an account of the history of the codex in which the text stands. At least another six books have been published in a little over a year since the appearance of the first translation.

[5] The classic pioneer was Adolf Deissmann (1927). More recently, the *New Documents Illustrating Early Christianity* series (Macquarie University 1981–) has added much to this domain.

[6] Bauer 1971 (originally appearing in German in 1934): 45.

[7] Jakab 2001, esp. chapter 8, "De la communauté chrétienne à l'église institutionnelle," pp. 175–214. Jakab is not skeptical about the possibility of knowing something about pre-Demetrian Christianity in Alexandria, only about the presence of an ecclesiastical hierarchical structure.

[8] Jakab's view probably exaggerates the situation. See Wipszycka 2006 for an argument that Eusebius's bishops were real, but were in a relationship of primus inter pares with respect to the rest of the Alexandrian presbyters.

[9] On Christian letters, see Wipszycka 1974. From the opening paragraph of her article, she recognizes the difficult role that the letters have been called on to play.

[10] Jakab 2001 throughout uses noncanonical Christian literature preserved only in later manuscripts (fourth century or later, that is) to argue for the nature of the community in which he supposes it was originally composed. But many of the attributions of works to an Alexandrian milieu are doubtful, and it is impossible to show that these works were actually circulating in the earlier period in Egypt.

[11] Jakab 2001: 47–48 believes (on what seems to me insufficient evidence) that what he regards as entirely a myth developed later than the bishop Dionysios (died 264).

[12] See Camplani 2004 for the "self-representation" of the Alexandrian episcopate.

[13] That logical connection again is one already made by Harnack 1908/1962: 476–77, although there he is talking about western provinces.

[14] Jakab 2001: 227. The logic of his claim (p. 58) that papyri found in the *chora* are evidence for Christianity in Alexandria but not in the Nile valley eludes me.

[15] The most thorough and thoughtful recent discussion of the difficulty of identifying Christians in documents is Choat 2006, with abundant bibliography; cf. my review in *Bulletin of the American Society of Papyrologists* 43 (2006): 205–9.

[16] Wipszycka 2001 gives a survey of the pre-Constantinian documentation of Christianity published in the previous twenty years, with bibliography concerning earlier studies. There is essentially nothing before the middle of the third century.

[17] Naldini 1968/1998 collects these letters. Wipszycka 1974: 221 argued that only forty-six of his ninety-seven should have been included in the volume. An extreme case is *P.Oxy.* XLII 3057, with an early palaeographical date assigned (first to second century) and a dubiously Christian character; see the arguments and bibliography in Ramelli 2000. See also Naldini 1995 for a supplementary discussion to his volume, in which he concludes (846), "Quanto alla cronologia, a parte la lettera del POxy 3057 del sec. I–II dal carattere cristiano problematico, la quasi-totalità dei nostri documenti è databile al sec. IV e al IV–V." (As for the chronology, apart from the letter POxy 3057, of the first–second century but uncertain Christian character, virtually all of our documents are datable to the fourth and fourth–fifth century.)

[18] Cf. Wipszycka 1974: 207: "chaque fois que ces sentiments et ces attitudes morales lui paraissent élevés et sympathiques, il pense qu'ils sont spécifiquement chrétiens." (Each time that these sentiments and moral attitudes seem to him lofty and congenial, he thinks that they are specifically Christian.)

[19] Roberts 1954, replying to Bell 1944, which Roberts describes as a "cool and critical survey of the private letters."

[20] Bauer 1971: 44–60, starting from Harnack's observation of how little we know about Egypt. A crucial passage (45) argues, "Now these sources were certainly seen and inspected, if not written, by churchmen. What reason could they have had for being silent about the origins of Christianity in such an important center as Alexandria if there had been something favorable to report?"

[21] Bauer himself, of course, observed that the distinction between orthodox and heretical was far from clear even in the third century (1971: 59); on early Christian pluralism, see more generally Ehrman 2003.

[22] http://www.trismegistos.org/ldab/, cited here as LDAB.

[23] *Proceedings of the British Academy* 43 (1957): 229–32; this is Bodl. MS Gr. Bibl. g.5 = LDAB 3083; Van Haelst 151; Turner Old Testament 97A.

[24] LDAB 3087; Van Haelst 179; Turner Old Testament 120.

[25] This is not only the criticism of Thiede (chapter 2); cf. Comfort and Barrett 1999: 40.

[26] Even in *P.Oxy.* I, Grenfell and Hunt dated the Gospel of Thomas (*P.Oxy.* 1) to ca. 200, a date revised to a few decades later in *P.Oxy.* IV 654 introd.

[27] LDAB 3086; Van Haelst 33; Turner Old Testament 24.

[28] *P.Ryl.* III 457; LDAB 2774; Van Haelst 462; Turner P52. Cf. Legras 2002: 88, not expressing an opinion.

[29] A. Schmidt, *Archiv für Papyrusforschung* 35 (1989): 11–12. Cf. *P.Bodmer* II, p. 17, making comparisons between that text, the Rylands fragment, and P.Egerton 2 (LDAB 4736, dated to II/III).

[30] Grenfell and Hunt's choice of the sayings of Jesus now called the Gospel of Thomas for the very first papyrus in the first volume of the *Oxyrhynchus Papyri* is emblematic.

[31] Hurtado 2006: 25 states without any documentation that "only about 1% of the estimated 500,000 manuscripts from this period have been published." This is certainly wrong. A total number on that order could refer only to preserved papyri including documents, and in that case the correct percentage would be more like 10 percent than 1 percent. No one knows how many unpublished literary papyri (i.e., book fragments) there are.

[32] For I/II, the percentage of Christians in 100 CE has been used. For the II century, percentages from the years 125, 150, and 175 have been averaged. For II/III, those from the years 175, 200, and 225 have been averaged.

Even if we used the percentage of Christians in 125, the expected number of books from the turn of the first to second centuries would not
be altered. The computation of the percentage for the second century
is more debatable, of course.

[33] We do not of course know how many grammarian's schools there were in
Egypt. Surely every nome metropolis had one, but so also did some
villages. If there were 100 of them altogether, each with 15 students
"graduating" per year, there might have been something like 4,000 to
5,000 Egyptian men with that level of education. The 100 Christians I
postulate to have been among them would have amounted to only 0.2
to 0.25 percent of this total (which may be too low). The speculative
character of all this will be evident, but the orders of magnitude seem
to me hard to escape.

Chapter II. Two Case Studies

[1] Thiede is absent from the bibliography and index of Hurtado 2006. In the
period immediately after Thiede's first publication of claims about the
Magdalen fragments, a number of articles not cited here appeared in
theological periodicals little read in papyrological circles; it is telling
that many of them appear in the *Bibliographie Papyrologique* with a
"non vidi."

[2] Vocke 1996 documents the fact that Thiede had no credentials as a papyrologist. He was, however, a member of the Association Internationale
de Papyrologues and duly received a memorial minute, delivered by
Cornelia Römer, at the XXV International Congress of Papyrology on
August 4, 2007.

[3] See Thiede 1984 and 1986. For the original claim, see O'Callaghan 1972. The
bibliography is extensive.

[4] For a recent discussion of the Villa of the Papyri, see Sider 2005.

[5] Rosenbaum 1987. Indeed, Rosenbaum's teacher Kurt Aland had from the start
already rejected O'Callaghan's identifications; see Aland 1974.

[6] See Aland and Aland 1989 (the remarks about differing types on p. 105, cited
by Thiede).

[7] Comfort 1999: 215 n. 4 complains about Thiede's misrepresentation and asserts
that he never changed his mind, although in my view Comfort 1999 is
more decisive than Comfort 1995 on the identity.

[8] See Comfort 1995 and 1999, and Comfort and Barrett 1999: 33–44, for accep-
tance of this view, which goes back originally to C. H. Roberts but was
fully defended only by Comfort and Skeat.

[9] Hurtado 2006: 56 n. 47 gives some bibliography on the debate over the separation of Christianity and Judaism—a major result of which is a widely

held view that such a separation was neither early, nor complete, nor irrevocable; cf. Becker and Reed 2003, 2nd ed. 2007.

10 Thiede is convinced that all second-century Christian texts would have been codices (p. 31), a view for which he offers very soft arguments and which is contradicted by the fact that only some categories of Christian texts were actually written in codex form this early; cf. chapter 4.

11 See O'Callaghan 1972; for a recent refutation of the proposal, see Enste 1999.

12 The reading of NNHΣ may be found 116 times in the New Testament and more elsewhere, and even that reading is insecure.

13 Most astonishing is the claim, p. 116, that this dating was only of secondary interest to Thiede! Comfort and Barrett 1999: 43 offer a weak argument from the reuse of P4 in the middle of the third century to buttress a compromise date of the middle of the second century. Cf. Comfort 1999: 217, mistakenly supposing that the use of an apostrophe between a doubled consonant points to a date ca. 150–200 for the flyleaf inscription with the title "according to Matthew" in P4.

14 See, for the Latin text of the Muratorian Canon, Lietzmann 1908: 8–11, lines 73–80: Pastorem vero nuperrime temporibus nostris in urbe Roma Hermias conscripsit sedente cathedra urbis Romae ecclesiae Pio episcopo fratre eius: et ideo legi cum quidem oportet, se publicare vero in ecclesia populo neque inter prophetas completo numero neque inter apostolos in fine temporum potest.

15 It is true that there has been an attempt to date the Muratorian Canon to a later period, but I have the impression that this attempt has not generally been accepted; see Ehrman 2003: 240–43 with 278 n. 27, giving references to some of the debate.

16 Carlini 1987; *P.Bodm.* XXXVIII, pp. 15ff.

CHAPTER III. THE ECONOMICS OF BOOK PRODUCTION

1 The development of this chapter has benefited from a paper by Brendan Haug in my graduate seminar at the University of California, Berkeley, during the fall 2005 semester, and discussion of that paper.

2 Boud'hors 2008.

3 Lauffer 1971: 120–21 (text), 217–18 (commentary).

4 The artaba of wheat weighed a little over 30 kg; the modius referred to here around 9 kg.

5 Mratschek 2000: 374 speaks of the New Testament as making up a third of the Bible. That is wrong. It is less than a fifth (146,618 words).

6 It is possible that the figure from 338–341 is a low price and the other closer to correct. The prices for papyrus from the first and second centuries

tend to suggest that the cost per roll was a higher fraction of the value of an artaba of wheat, perhaps more like one-sixth to one-fourth.

[7] See Bagnall 2002b for a recent discussion of commodity prices.

[8] *P.Oxy.Census*, pp. 22–23 with references.

[9] On monks' economic activities, see most recently Wipszycka 2007b with references to earlier discussion.

[10] The classic study is Wipszycka 1975.

[11] *Later Roman Empire* 902–03, cited by Hübner 2005: 219.

[12] For the largest of all urban centers, Rome, Eusebius (*Hist. Eccl.* 6.43.11) gives a count for the mid–third century, including 41 *presbyteroi*, 7 deacons, and 7 subdeacons.

[13] Even that change was not immediate. Paper, as a handmade product, was still relatively expensive in the premodern period: Bloom 2001: 74–85, esp. 79 on prices. Paper was introduced into Egypt in the ninth century, manufactured there only from the tenth.

[14] Although its early history is far less solidly attested than sometimes thought; cf. Jakab 2001: 91–106 on the problem of the "school of Alexandria" and his chapters 5–7 on Pantainos, Clement, and Origen.

[15] Individual cases of wealthy Christians in Alexandria form no basis for generalization about the Alexandrian Christian community as a whole, let alone Christians in the rest of Egypt.

[16] Some information on Origen's books is provided by Eusebius; see Carriker 2003.

[17] See Bagnall 2005 for a more detailed discussion of this subject.

[18] It should be said that it is by no means impossible that some of these individuals came from families that had held priestly status. Even though the temples were hardly important sources of wealth in the Severan period, some priests in the first two centuries of Roman rule received a Greek education as well as traditional Egyptian learning.

Chapter IV. The Spread of the Codex

[1] The term seems to me, for all its potential ambiguity, more felicitous than the term "sacred" used by Crisci 2003.

[2] See O'Donnell 1998 and Johnson 2000 for these larger issues about the interaction of technology and cultural practices.

[3] Another form of misleading analysis has been that seeking to show that there are fundamental differences between Christian and non-Christian books. Barker 2007 has shown that when like is compared with like— Christian and non-Christian codices—the differences are minimal. That argument has important implications for the difference between the codex and the book roll as types of book.

[4] See Hurtado 2006: 17–24 for a recent synopsis of the works surviving in the early fragments and some bibliography on questions of emergent canonicity.

[5] The one exception is *BKT* IX 22, a fragment of a codex dated by the editor second/third century and identified as "Prose (Christian Text?)." The possible identification of the text as Christian rests on two restorations printed in the text. In both cases, the restorations are gratuitous. There are numerous other possibilities, even if this should be a Christian text. If it were, nothing excludes the possibility that it belongs to a noncanonical work of scripture; but equally, it could be (for example) part of an astrological handbook.

[6] Reedited in *Zeitschrift für Papyrologie und Epigraphik* 92 (1992): 243–47.

[7] This point is made by Hurtado 2006: 57.

[8] Hurtado 2006: 53–61 gives a useful general discussion of the codex versus roll question, taking matters somewhat later than I do here in dealing with possible exceptions.

[9] The eventual decline of the use of papyrus compared with parchment is discussed by Crisci 2003: 84–85.

[10] Roberts and Skeat 1983. Although this is a "practical" explanation, it was advanced in opposition to more general claims for the practical advantages of the codex; see Hurtado 2006: 63–66, who agrees in dismissing these advantages. The proposal of Eldon Epp (1997) and others, stimulated by a suggestion of Michael McCormick, to see convenience in travel as decisive is another hypothesis essentially based on practicality; cf. the discussion of Hurtado 2006: 74–77.

[11] http://ccat.sas.upenn.edu/rs/rak/jewishpap.html.

[12] See Hurtado 2006: 61–63 on this matter, with a similar conclusion.

[13] Hurtado 2006: 70–74 also rejects both proposals, although the Pauline hypothesis less decisively than the gospel one. See his treatment for a bibliography on the debate concerning these views.

[14] There is much work to be done on this question. Turner 1977: 102–85 collected much of the data, but it is evident there how much information is unknown.

[15] I shall discuss this matter in more detail in the book deriving from my Sather lectures, "Everyday Writing in the Graeco-Roman East."

[16] Dieleman 2005. I defer to another place a detailed analysis of the dates of the rest of the magical papyri. See broadly on the subject Brashear 1995 with a full bibliography.

[17] See, for example, Gamble 1995: 50–53.

[18] Cf. modern debate (in Gamble 1995) on whether the scriptures are literature.

[19] I am excluding LDAB 4305 = *P.Hamb.* II 134; this has a rhetorical piece or novel written on the back of an account and is clearly not a codex

leaf. I also exclude LDAB 4444, stated to be a codex. This is an unillustrated fragment of an unknown drama for which the editor gives no evidence that it is in fact from a codex (*PSI* II 134), saying that the verso is blank. LDAB 6833 (P.Stras.inv. 1352) is also listed as a codex, but this school exercise may simply be a single leaf rather than from a codex. Its date is also very uncertain; cf. Cribiore 1996: no. 280 with pl. XXXIII. Cf. Barker 2007 for the need to see codices, both Christian and non-Christian, as something different from book rolls.

[20] Hurtado 2006: 50 with n. 23 adds to this count a number of other astronomical papyri (LDAB 7242, 7269, 7298, 7299, 8141), but this is misleading; these are all dated in LDAB as first to third or first to fourth century and thus no use. Almost all of them, in fact, belong to an archive of texts thrown on the rubbish at Oxyrhynchus in the early fourth century: see Jones 1999: I 59. Hurtado also lists LDAB 3910 (now 3910+7052), but that is first-to-second century, not simply first; and LDAB 10361 (now = 10640), but that is fourth century and thus irrelevant. There is thus a great deal less evidence for first-century use of the codex than Hurtado would lead one to believe.

[21] I note that Hurtado 2006: 80–83 also ends without a definite answer, asserting mainly the importance of the question.

[22] Roberts and Skeat 1983: 57–58, quoted by Hurtado 2006: 71.

[23] Grafton and Williams 2006: 71–72 compare Rome to Alexandria at this stage. Even if their model of a presbyter-governed church were correct, however, it would not exclude the possibility of decisive action of the kind that centralized adoption of the codex would require.

Bibliography

Aland, Kurt. 1974. "Neue neutestamentliche Papyri III." *New Testament Studies* 20: 357–81.

———. 1976. *Repertorium der griechischen christlichen Papyri* (Patristische Texte und Studien 18). Berlin.

Aland, Kurt, and Barbara Aland. 1989. *Der Text des Neuen Testaments*, 2nd ed. Stuttgart.

Bagnall, Roger S. 1985. *Currency and Inflation in Fourth Century Egypt* (BASP Suppl. 5). Atlanta.

———. 1993. *Egypt in Late Antiquity*. Princeton.

———. 1995. *Reading Papyri, Writing Social History*. London.

———. 2002a. "Public Administration and the Documentation of Roman Panopolis," in *Perspectives on Panopolis*, ed. A. Egberts, B. P. Muhs, and J. van der Vliet (Papyrologica Lugduno-Batava 31), 1–12. Leiden; reprinted in *Hellenistic and Roman Egypt: Sources and Approaches* (Aldershot 2006), chapter 19.

———. 2002b. "The Effects of Plague: Model and Evidence." *JRA* 15: 114–20.

———. 2005. "Linguistic Change and Religious Change: Thinking about the Temples of the Fayoum in the Roman Period," in *Christianity and Monasticism in the Fayoum Oasis*, ed. G. Gabra, 11–19. Cairo.

Bagnall, Roger S., and Raffaella Cribiore. 2006. *Women's Letters from Ancient Egypt, 300 BC–AD 800*. Ann Arbor.

Barker, D. C. 2007. "A Comparative Analysis of Secular and Christian Codices from Second Century Oxyrhynchus." Paper read at the 25th International Congress of Papyrology, Ann Arbor, July 31.

Bauer, Walter. 1971. *Orthodoxy and Heresy in Earliest Christianity*, ed. R. A. Kraft and G. Krodel from the 2nd German ed. Philadelphia.

Becker, Adam, and Annette Reed. 2003, 2nd ed. 2007. *The Ways That Never Parted: Jews and Christians in Late Antiquity and the Early Middle Ages*. Tübingen/Minneapolis.

Bell, H. I. 1944. "Evidences of Christianity in Egypt during the Roman Period." *Harvard Theological Review* 37: 185–208.

Bloom, Jonathan. 2001. *Paper before Print.* New Haven.

Boud'hors, Anne. 2008. "Copie et circulation des livres dans la région thébaine," in *Actes du colloque "Thèbes et sa région aux époques hellénistique, romaine et byzantine" (Bruxelles, 2–3 décembre 2005),* ed. A. Delattre and P. Heilporn. Brussels.

Brashear, William. 1995. "The Greek Magical Papyri, an Introduction and Survey: Annotated Bibliography, 1928–1994." *Aufstieg und Niedergang der römischen Welt* II 18.5: 3380–3684.

Camplani, Alberto. 2004. "L'autorappresentazione dell'episcopato di Alessandria tra IV e V secolo: questioni di metodo." *Annali di storia dell'esegesi* 21: 147–85.

Carlini, Antonio. 1983. "P. Michigan 130 (inv. 44-H) e il problema dell'unicità di redazione del Pastore di Erma." *Parola del Passato* 38 fasc. 208: 29–37.

———. 1987. "La tradizione testuale del Pastore di Erma e i nuovi papiri," in *Le strade del testo,* ed. G. Cavallo, 23–43. Bari.

———. 1992. "Testimone e testo: Il problema della datazione di PIand I 4 del Pastore di Erma." *Studi Classici e Orientali* 42: 17–30.

Carriker, Andrew J. 2003. *The Library of Eusebius of Caesarea.* Leiden.

Charlesworth, Scott D. 2007. "T. C. Skeat, P[64+67] and P[4], and the Problem of Fibre Orientation in Codicological Reconstruction." Paper presented at the 25th International Congress of Papyrology, Ann Arbor, July 31.

Choat, Malcolm. 2006. *Belief and Cult in Fourth-Century Papyri* (Studia Antiqua Australiensia 1). Turnhout.

Comfort, Philip W. 1995. "Exploring the Common Identification of Three New Testament Manuscripts: P4, P64 and P67." *Tyndale Bulletin* 46: 43–54.

———. 1999. "New Reconstructions and Identifications of New Testament Papyri." *Novum Testamentum* 41: 214–30.

Comfort, Philip W., and D. P. Barrett. 1999. *The Complete Text of the Earliest New Testament Manuscripts.* Grand Rapids.

Cribiore, Raffaella. 1996. *Writing, Teachers, and Students in Graeco-Roman Egypt* (American Studies in Papyrology 36). Atlanta.

———. 2001. *Gymnastics of the Mind: Greek Education in Hellenistic and Roman Egypt.* Princeton.

Crisci, Edoardo. 2003. "Papiro e pergamena nella produzione libraria in Oriente fra IV e VIII secolo d.C. Materiali e reflessioni." *Segno e testo* 1: 79–127.

Cuvigny, Hélène. 2009. "The Finds of Papyri: the Archaeology of Papyrology," in *The Oxford Handbook of Papyrology,* ed. R. S. Bagnall, 30–58. Oxford.

Davis, Stephen. 2004. *The Early Coptic Papacy: The Egyptian Church and Its Leadership in Late Antiquity* (The Popes of Egypt 1). Cairo and New York.

Deissmann, Adolf. 1927. *Light from the Ancient East: The New Testament Illustrated by Recently Discovered Texts of the Graeco-Roman World.* London.

Dieleman, Jacco. 2005. *Priests, Tongues, and Rites: The London-Leiden Magical Manuscripts and Translation in Egyptian Ritual (100–300 CE)* (Religions in the Graeco-Roman World 153). Leiden.

Ehrman, Bart D. 2003. *Lost Christianities: The Battles for Scripture and the Faiths We Never Knew.* Oxford.

Emmel, Stephen. 1998. "The Christian Book in Egypt: Innovation and the Coptic Tradition," in *The Bible as Book: The Manuscript Tradition,* ed. J. L. Sharpe and Kimberly van Kampen, 35–43. London.

Enste, Stefan. 1999. "Qumran-Fragment 7Q5 ist nicht Markus 6, 52–53." *Zeitschrift für Papyrologie und Epigraphik* 126: 189–94.

Epp, Eldon J. 1997. "The Codex and Literacy in Early Christianity and at Oxyrhynchus," in *Critical Review of Books in Religion 1997,* ed. C. Prebisch, 15–37. Atlanta.

Förster, Hans. 2002. "Heilige Namen in Heiligen Texten." *Antike Welt* 33: 321–24.

Fowden, Garth. 1993. *The Egyptian Hermes: A Historical Approach to the Late Pagan Mind.* Princeton.

Gamble, Harry Y. 1995. *Books and Readers in the Early Church: A History of Early Christian Texts.* New Haven.

Gascou, Jean. 1989. "Les codices documentaires Égyptiens," in *Les débuts du codex,* ed. A. Blanchard, 71–101. Turnhout.

Grafton, Anthony, and Megan Williams. 2006. *Christianity and the Transformation of the Book: Origen, Eusebius, and the Library of Caesarea.* Cambridge, Mass.

Harnack, Adolf. 1908/1962. *The Mission and Expansion of Christianity in the First Three Centuries,* trans. J. Moffatt. New York.

Hopkins, Keith. 1998. "Christian Number and Its Implications." *Journal of Early Christian Studies* 6: 185–226.

Hübner, Sabine. 2005. *Der Klerus in der Gesellschaft des spätantiken Kleinasiens* (Altertumswissenschaftliches Kolloquium 15). Stuttgart.

Hunger, Herbert H. 1960. "Zur Datierung des Papyrus Bodmer II." *Anzeiger der Österreichischen Akademie der Wissenschaften, philosophisch-historische Klasse* 4: 12–23.

Hurtado, Larry W. 2006. *The Earliest Christian Artifacts: Manuscripts and Christian Origins.* Grand Rapids.

Jakab, Attila. 2001. *Ecclesia alexandrina. Evolution sociale et institutionelle du christianisme alexandrin (IIe et IIIe siècles)* (Christianismes antiques 1). Bern.

Jaroš, Karl. 2001. "Ein neues Fragment des Hebräerbriefes." *Antike Welt* 32: 271–73.

Johnson, William. 2000. "Toward a Sociology of Reading in Classical Antiquity." *American Journal of Philology* 121: 593–627.

Jones, Alexander. 1999. *Astronomical Papyri from Oxyrhynchus*, 2 vols.
Philadelphia.

Kasser, Rudolf, Marvin Meyer, and Gregor Wurst. 2006. *The Gospel of Judas:
From Codex Tchacos*. Washington, D.C.

Kim, Y. K. 1988. "Palaeographical Dating of P^{46} to the Later First Century."
Biblica 69: 248–57.

Koenen, Ludwig. 1974. "Ein Mönch als Berufsschreiber. Zur Buchproduktion
im 5./6. Jahrhundert," in *Festschrift zum 150 jährigen Bestehen des Ber-
liner Ägyptischen Museums*, 347–54. Berlin.

Kotsifou, Chrysi. 2007. "Books and Book Production in the Monastic Communities of Byzantine Egypt," in *The Early Christian Book*, ed. W. E.
Klingshirn and L. Safran, 48–66. Washington, D.C.

Krosney, Herbert. 2006. *The Lost Gospel: The Quest for the Gospel of Judas
Iscariot*. Washington, D.C.

Lauffer, Siegfried. 1971. *Diokletians Preisedikt*. Berlin.

Legras, Bernard. 2002. *Lire en Égypte: d'Alexandre à l'Islam*. Paris.

Lietzmann, H. 1908. *Das Muratorische Fragment und die monarchianischen
Prologe zu den Evangelien*, 2nd ed. Bonn.

Luijendijk, AnneMarie. Forthcoming. *"Greetings in the Lord": Early Christians
and the Oxyrhynchus Papyri* (Harvard Theological Studies 59). Cambridge, Mass.

MacMullen, Ramsay. 1989. "The Preacher's Audience (AD 350–400)." *Journal of
Theological Studies* 40: 503–11.

Meeks, Wayne A. 1983. *The First Urban Christians*. New Haven.

Meyer, Elizabeth A. 2004. *Legitimacy and Law in the Roman World:* Tabulae *in
Roman Belief and Practice*. Cambridge.

Mratschek, Sigrid. 2000. "*Codices vestri nos sumus*: Bücherkult und Bücherpreise
in der christlichen Spätantike," in *Hortus litterarum antiquarum, Festschrift für Hans Armin Gärtner zum 70. Geburtstag*, ed. A. Haltenhoff
and F.-H. Mutschler, 369–80. Heidelberg.

Naldini, Mario. 1968/1998. *Il cristianesimo in Egitto. Lettere private nei papiri dei
secoli II–IV*, 2nd ed. Fiesole.

———. 1995. "Nuove testimonianze cristiane nei papiri greco-egizi." *Augustinianum* 35: 831–46.

Nongbi, Brent. 2005. "The Use and Abuse of P52: Papyrological Pitfalls in
the Dating of the Fourth Gospel." *Harvard Theological Review* 98:
23–48.

O'Callaghan, José. 1972. "¿Papiros neotestamentarios en la cueva 7 de Qumran?"
Biblica 53: 91–100.

O'Donnell, James J. 1998. *Avatars of the Word: From Papyrus to Cyberspace*.
Cambridge, Mass.

Papathomas, Amphilochios. 2000. "A New Testimony to the Letter to the Hebrews." *Journal of Graeco-Roman Christianity and Judaism* 1: 18–23.

Passoni dell'Acqua, Anna. 2003. "Biblica in Papyris III (2002)." *Papyrologica Lupiensia* 12: 201–216.

Preisendanz, Karl. 1933. *Papyrusfunde und Papyrusforschung*. Leipzig.

Ramelli, Ilaria. 2000. "Una delle più antiche lettere cristiane extracanoniche?" *Aegyptus* 80: 169–88.

Roberts, C. H. 1954. "Early Christianity in Egypt." *Journal of Egyptian Archaeology* 40: 92–96.

Roberts, C. H., and T. C. Skeat. 1983. *The Birth of the Codex*. London.

Rosenbaum, Hans-Udo. 1987. "Cave 7Q! Gegen die erneute Inanspruchnahme des Qumran-Fragments 7Q5 als Bruchstück der ältesten Evangelien-Handschrift." *Biblische Zeitschrift* 51: 189–205.

Schmelz, Georg. 2002. *Kirchliche Amtsträger in spätantiken Ägypten nach der Aussagen der griechischen und koptischen Papyri und Ostraka* (Archiv für Papyrusforschung, Beiheft 13). Munich.

Sider, David. 2005. *The Library of the Villa dei Papiri at Herculaneum*. Malibu.

Skeat, Theodore C. 1982. "The Length of the Standard Papyrus-Roll and the Cost-Advantage of the Codex." *Zeitschrift für Papyrologie und Epigraphik* 45: 169–76.

———. 1994. "The Origin of the Christian Codex." *Zeitschrift für Papyrologie und Epigraphik* 102: 263–68.

———. 1997. "The Oldest Manuscript of the Four Gospels?" *New Testament Studies* 43: 1–34.

Stanton, Graham. 1995. *Gospel Truth? New Light on Jesus and the Gospels*. London.

Stark, Rodney. 1996. *The Rise of Christianity: A Sociologist Reconsiders History*. Princeton.

Thiede, Carsten P. 1984. "7Q. Eine Rückkehr zu den neutestamentlichen Papyrusfragmenten in der siebten Höhle von Qumran." *Biblica* 65: 538–59.

———. 1986. *Die älteste Evangelien-Handschrift? Das Markus-Fragment von Qumran und die Anfänge der schriftlichen Überlieferung des Neuen Testaments*. Wuppertal.

———. 1995. "Papyrus Magdalen Greek 17 (Gregory-Aland P⁶⁴). A Reappraisal." *Zeitschrift für Papyrologie und Epigraphik* 105: 13–20.

Thiede, Carsten P., and Matthew D'Ancona. 1996. *Eyewitness to Jesus*. New York.

Treu, Kurt. 1973/1991. "Die Bedeutung des Griechischen für die Juden im römischen Reich." *Kairos* NF 15: 123–44; English translation (1991) available (by W. Adler with R. Kraft) at ftp://ftp.lehigh.edu/pub/listserv/ioudaios-l/Articles/ktreu.

Turner, Eric G. 1977. *The Typology of the Early Codex*. Philadelphia.

Van Haelst, Joseph. 1976. *Catalogue des papyrus littéraires juifs et chrétiens*. Paris.

Van Minnen, Peter. 1986. "A Change of Names in Roman Egypt after AD 202? A Note on P.Amst. I 72." *Zeitschrift für Papyrologie und Epigraphik* 62: 87–92.

———. Forthcoming. "The Future of Papyrology," in *The Oxford Handbook of Papyrology*, ed. R. S. Bagnall, 644–60. Oxford.

Vocke, H. 1996. "Papyrus Magdalen 17—weitere Argumente gegen die Frühdatierung des angeblichen Jesus-Papyrus." *Zeitschrift für Papyrologie und Epigraphik* 113: 153–57.

Wachtel, Karl. 1996. "P64/67: Fragmente des Matthäusevangeliums aus dem 1. Jahrhundert?" *Zeitschrift für Papyrologie und Epigraphik* 107: 73–80.

Wipszycka, Ewa. 1974. "Remarques sur les lettres privées chrétiennes des III–IVe siècles. A propos d'un livre de M. Naldini." *Journal of Juristic Papyrology* 18: 203–21.

———. 1975. "Les terres de la congrégation pachômienne dans une liste de payements pour les apora," in *Le monde grec: pensée, littérature, histoire, documents. Hommages à Claire Préaux*, ed. J. Bingen, G. Cambier, and G. Nachtergael, 625–36. Brussels.

———. 1996. *Études sur le christianisme dans l'Égypte de l'antiquité tardive* (Studia Ephemeridis Augustinianum 52). Rome.

———. 2000. "The Nag Hammadi Library and the Monks." *Journal of Juristic Papyrology* 30: 179–91.

———. 2001. "Les papyrus documentaires concernant l'Église d'avant le tournant constantinien. Un bilan des vingt dernières années." *Atti del XXII Congresso Internazionale di Papirologia* (Florence 2001) 2: 1307–30.

———. 2006. "The Origins of the Monarchic Episcopate in Egypt." *Adamantius* 12: 71–89.

———. 2007a. "The Institutional Church," in *Egypt in the Byzantine World, 300–700*, ed. R. S. Bagnall, 331–49. Cambridge.

———. 2007b. "Les formes institutionnelles et les formes d'activité économique du monachisme égyptien," in *Foundations of Power and Conflicts of Authority in Late-Antique Monasticism*, ed. A. Camplani and G. Filoramo (Orientalia Lovaniensia Analecta 157), 109–54. Leuven.

———. Forthcoming. *Moines et communautés monastiques en Égypte, IVe–VIIe siècles* (Journal of Juristic Papyrology Suppl. 11). Warsaw.

Index of Subjects

Index of Papyrological Texts Discussed